Seattle

YESTERDAY & TODAY ™

J. Kingston Pierce

WEST
SIDE
PUBLISHING

J. Kingston Pierce is a veteran journalist and magazine editor. His previous books include *San Francisco, You're History!*, *America's Historic Trails with Tom Bodett*, *Eccentric Seattle*, and *San Francisco: Yesterday & Today*™. He has also written for *Salon* and *Travel & Leisure* and is the editor of an award-winning crime-fiction blog, The Rap Sheet (http//www.therapsheet.blogspot.com). Pierce lives with his wife in Seattle.

Robert Holmes is a photographer who has traveled the world for major magazines, including *National Geographic*, *Travel Holiday*, *Life*, *Time*, *Travel + Leisure*, *GEO*, and *Islands.* He was the first person to twice receive the Travel Photographer of the Year Award from the Society of American Travel Writers. You can learn more about Holmes at www.robertholmesphotography.com.

ISBN-13: 978-1-4127-1577-5
ISBN-10: 1-4127-1577-6

Manufactured in China.

8 7 6 5 4 3 2 1

Library of Congress Control Number: 2008942458

Above: The Space Needle is a prominent fixture in the Seattle skyline.

Contents

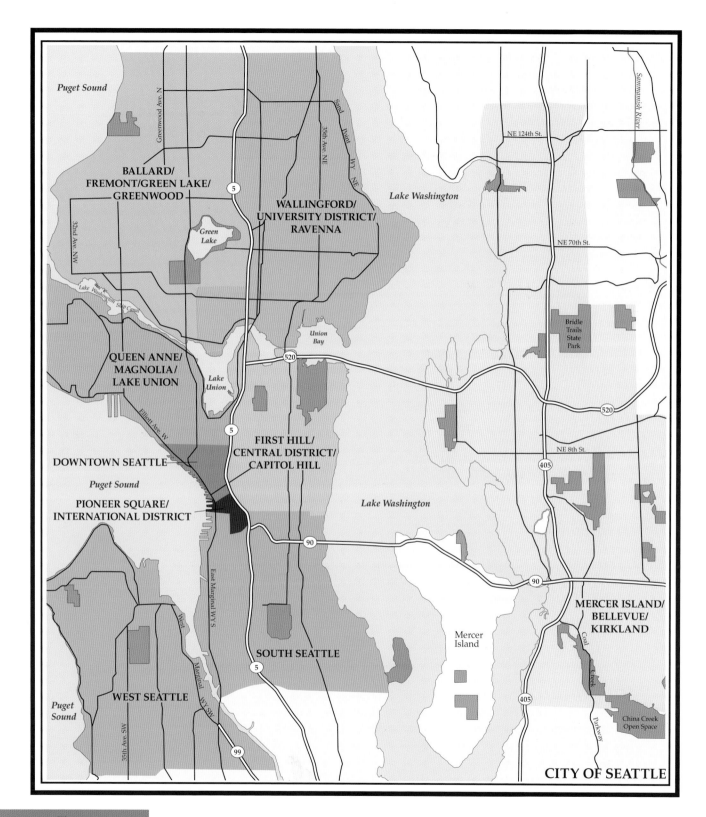

Puget Sound

BALLARD/
FREMONT/GREEN LAKE/
GREENWOOD

Greenwood Ave. N

32nd Ave. NW

Green Lake

Lake Washington Ship Canal

WALLINGFORD/
UNIVERSITY DISTRICT/
RAVENNA

Sand Point Wy. NE

35th Ave. NE

Lake Washington

NE 124th St.

NE 70th St.

Sammamish River

Bridle Trails State Park

QUEEN ANNE/
MAGNOLIA/
LAKE UNION

Elliott Ave. W

Lake Union

Union Bay

520

520

405

NE 8th St.

DOWNTOWN SEATTLE

FIRST HILL/
CENTRAL DISTRICT/
CAPITOL HILL

Puget Sound

Lake Washington

PIONEER SQUARE/
INTERNATIONAL DISTRICT

East Marginal Wy S

90

90

MERCER ISLAND/
BELLEVUE/
KIRKLAND

405

Cool Creek

SOUTH SEATTLE

Marginal Wy SW

Mercer Island

WEST SEATTLE

35th Ave. SW

West

Puget Sound

99

Parkway

China Creek Open Space

CITY OF SEATTLE

A PLACE IN THE SUN...
ER, RAIN

My, how things have changed. In the 1937 film *Stage Door,* future TV star Lucille Ball appeared as a wannabe starlet from Seattle, who was living in a Broadway boardinghouse with other aspiring actresses. When one of her housemates, played by Eve Arden, remarked acerbically, "I thought the people out there lived in trees," the young Ball shot back: "Only in the summertime." It was probably easier then, just three decades after the Klondike Gold Rush, to joke about backwoods Seattleites. And in fact, there were stories told of one man actually residing in a giant cedar stump north of the city.

More than 70 years later, the image of Seattle dwellers is quite different. Now, they are pictured as caffeine-jagged high-tech workers, probably living on house-boats (blame *Sleepless in Seattle* for that cliché) and whiling away their weekends hiking mountain trails or fishing for their salmon dinners.

Neither picture is entirely accurate, of course. As is the case with most large cities, it's difficult to develop an overarching characterization of Seattle's population. Hiking boots and wool shirts sell well in this place; it's no coincidence that outdoor outfitters Eddie Bauer and REI were both founded here. But Seattleites also purchase more sunglasses per capita than the residents of any other U.S. city,

which kind of puts the kibosh on stories about it raining all the time here. (The truth, as any local will insist, is that it only rains on vacation days.) And the lumbermen who were always trying to date Lucille Ball's *Stage Door* character are pretty thin on the ground in the 21st century, which is also the unfortunate case with the old-growth timber they once harvested.

Since its founding in the 1850s, Seattle has traveled the unpredictable road from *terra incognita* (a spot so remote that one mid-19th-century ship sailed up here from San Francisco looking for icebergs to use for cooling drinks on the Barbary Coast) to being celebrated for its "liv-ability" and cultural attributes. Even

Above: Captain George Vancouver

Left: A map of Seattle neighborhoods

Right: East on Pike Street from First Avenue, circa 1916

Space Needle—without knowing about the roles designer Elmer H. Fisher, landscaper John C. Olmsted, and engineer Reginald H. Thomson played in creating the urban canvas on which these comparatively recent creations could shine.

Over the years, the Pacific Northwest's largest city has fielded its share of criticism. The *San Francisco Chronicle* once knocked it as "an old gold-mining stopover peopled by too many boring Canadians to have any real style." Comedian Jerry Seinfeld quipped that "Seattle is a moisturizing pad disguised as a city." Locals have learned to take it all in stride and occasionally encourage talk of moss growing between their toes and floating bridges permanently clogged with cars. It's a small price to pay if it dissuades others from moving here.

Below: East on Pike Street from First Avenue, circa 1930

most Seattleites are familiar with only small parts of the city's story. They may know it as the birthplace of Microsoft cofounder Bill Gates, the former home of martial-arts star Bruce Lee, and the place where musician Kurt Cobain committed suicide. But they might be unfamiliar with its status as the birthplace of gas stations. They may realize that British Captain George Vancouver explored Puget Sound in 1792 but be

unaware of the city's role in opening Alaska to the world. Perhaps they have heard that trumpeter-conductor Quincy Jones and singer Judy Collins both got their starts here but know nothing about once-famous musical venues such as Birdland or the Trianon Ballroom. Chances are they recognize downtown's modern architectural landmarks—the Seattle Art Museum, Rem Koolhaas's geometrically dynamic public library, the

Right: The Space Needle and skyline circa 1962 *(left)* and present day *(right)*

Pioneer Square/International District

THE WELL-ROUNDED SQUARE

Seattle can claim no natural center—no majestic plaza or rolling green to which residents invariably gravitate in times of revelry or sorrow. Instead, its urban core boasts two distinct and beloved poles. On the north is Pike Place Market, a quirky, rambling hive of commercialism that dates to 1907. About half a mile south of Pike Place Market is Pioneer Square, a protected historical district more than 80 acres in size, stuffed with wonderful low-rise Victorian brick edifices. Pioneer Square was Seattle's original downtown. However, things weren't supposed to work out that way.

Led by settlers Arthur and David Denny, Carson Boren, and William Bell, two dozen adults and children from the Midwest reached this rainy, forested outback by sailing ship on November 13, 1851. At first, they tried homesteading what's now scenic Alki Point, in West Seattle, on the opposite, western shore of Elliott Bay. But it didn't take them long to realize that their new colony was not destined to become the metropolis they had imagined: "New York *Alki*," or—translated from Chinook jargon—"New York by and by." Its shallow, windy harbor and distant tree line made Alki Point a less than ideal anchorage for vessels intending to load up with this area's single marketable resource: timber, much in demand down the West Coast in booming San

Francisco. So the settlers begrudgingly packed together what remained of their worldly possessions and headed east across the bay to begin anew in the vicinity of today's Pioneer Square.

Even then, it took a latecomer—a physician and merchant from Ohio, David "Doc" Maynard—to really get matters moving here. Maynard instigated the surveying of streets and convinced another midwesterner, Henry Yesler, to construct his steam-powered sawmill on the east side of Elliott Bay, rather than at Alki. To secure that deal, Maynard, Boren, and Arthur Denny had to give Yesler 320 acres of old-growth timberland above the town, plus a waterfront lot and a ribbon of property linking the

Above: David "Doc" Maynard

Left: Seattle in 1878, as seen from Denny Hill

two, down which oxen could (with great difficulty) drag felled evergreens. That strip was known for years as Mill Street and is now Yesler Way; but early on it earned the nickname "skid road," later mangled into "skid row," an early 20th-century insult applied to neighborhoods that had fallen on hard times.

Above: This 1899 ad invites Seattleites to an illustrated lecture on the Alaska and Klondike gold fields.

By the end of the 1880s, Seattle looked to be on its way up, having sprouted shops, newspapers, a territorial university, and an elegant opera house on Front Street (now First Avenue). Thanks to the university's president, Asa Mercer, the town had even overcome a severe shortage of marriage-age women by importing some from Massachusetts—a most curious convergence of commerce and courtship celebrated in the 1960s TV series *Here Come the Brides*.

GONE TO BLAZES

Unfortunately, fire struck in the summer of 1889, reducing Seattle's historic downtown—including its nascent Chinatown section—to cinders in just over half a day. British writer Rudyard Kipling, who happened to visit Elliott Bay by steamship soon after the blaze, later recalled the scene in *From Sea to Sea and Other Sketches: Letters of Travel* (1925):

In the heart of the business quarters there was a horrible black smudge, as though a Hand had come down and rubbed the place smooth. I know now what being wiped out means. The smudge seemed to be about a mile long, and its blackness was relieved by tents in which men were doing business with the wreck of the stock they had saved. There were shouts and counter-shouts from the steamer to the temporary wharf, which was laden with shingles for roofing, chairs, trunks, provision-boxes, and all the lath and string arrangements out of which a western town is made.

REBIRTH

Those supplies would come in handy as the city hurried to rebuild. Over the next few years, a new, bigger, more organized Seattle took its place upon the ashes of the old. It vied for regional supremacy with Tacoma, its chief Puget Sound rival, and finally won a much-desired transcontinental railway connection. It was devastated by the Panic of 1893, which sent local real-estate values plummeting

by 80 percent and closed hundreds of small businesses all over King County. But Seattle climbed back fast with the advent of the Klondike Gold Rush (1897–1899), during which Elliott Bay became the frenzied transit point for miners heading north to the precious metal-bearing rivers of northwestern Canada and returning with their pockets full of gold dust. By 1909, when Seattle hosted the first of its two world's fairs, it could again claim to be "the boomingest place on earth."

There was a downside to that boom, though. As the city grew, its energy moved northward into more modern business towers and shopping areas. During the mid-20th century, Pioneer Square and its adjacent Asian quarter took on an abandoned air. So decrepit did Seattle's original downtown become, that in 1966 city officials proposed doing what even fire had once failed to accomplish: eliminating Pioneer Square to make room for new parking lots and office termitaries. Fortunately, supporters stepped in to buy and refurbish some of the area's monumental edifices, and in 1970, Pioneer Square was designated as the city's first historic district. Though neither of these areas can claim to be the center of Seattle, Pioneer Square and Pike Place Market remain the city's heart and soul.

Right: View of Seattle from Beacon Hill, circa 1881; Yesler's Mill is visible at the end of the peninsula.

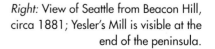

PIONEER PLACE

Seattle's earliest intersection of any consequence was at Front Street (which later became First Avenue) and Yesler Way. For many years, this junction was known as "Yesler's Corner" because so much of the property there was owned by Henry Yesler. He built a sawmill near that crossroads; the wharf where his men loaded colossal logs onto ships bound for West Coast ports marked the waterfront end of Yesler Way.

Prior to the Great Fire of 1889, this place was an awkward confluence of thorough-fares, the result of a disagreement between Doc Maynard and Arthur Denny, who had been given joint responsibility for platting the new town's grid. In what seemed like a logical plan, Maynard parceled out real estate south of Yesler Way in a north–south direction parallel to the shoreline. Denny followed the same practice—the only problem was that the shoreline itself veered off to the northwest at Yesler Way. Both men were stubborn, with neither willing to accept the other's platting, so downtown Seattle was left with a misalignment of streets. Until the 1890s, what are now First Avenue and First Avenue South weren't even one continuous roadway. Instead, anyone traveling along both had to make a half-block-long connecting jog at Yesler Way.

It was at Front and Yesler that architect William Boone's Yesler-Leary Building (left, circa 1888) was raised in the early 1880s. Boone, who'd previously practiced in northern California, based his Victorian design on San Francisco's original Phelan Block.

Pioneer Building

Following the Great Fire of 1889, the city scrubbed Yesler's Corner from the map and bent Front Street to connect with what had been Commercial Street, creating today's lengthy First Avenue. The leftover empty triangle at First and Yesler became a park. Architect Elmer H. Fisher was commissioned by businessman-turned-politician Henry Yesler to create what is today the much-loved Pioneer Building. With its rusticated stone base, Roman entrance archway, and cast-iron bay windows, the Pioneer was considered so remarkable that even the American Institute of Architects in Washington, D.C., took notice, labeling it "the finest building west of Chicago." The Pioneer Building was completed after Yesler's death in 1892. In the photo, the six-story Pioneer Building appears on the right, with the ten-story French Renaissance chateaux-style Lowman Building (raised by Yesler's businessman nephew) on the far left.

Pioneer Place Park

Pioneer Place Park *(left),* as the tree-shaded triangle in front of the Pioneer Building is known, was developed in 1893. It features a fountain, sculpted by James A. Wehn and topped by a bust of Chief Sealth. Nearby is a cast-iron-and-glass pergola, designed by architect Julian Everett. The pergola was originally a streetcar station with a pretentious underground restroom (long ago closed) that was built for the benefit of visitors to Seattle's 1909 World's Fair. The park's main attraction, though, is a 60-foot totem pole. It's actually the second such pillar on this site. The initial one came from a Tlingit Indian village on Alaska's Tongass Island. In 1899, a "goodwill" party sent north by the local chamber of commerce and the *Seattle Post-Intelligencer* stopped at the Alaskan Indian village while its residents were off fishing. Enchanted by a line of totems bordering the beach, the visitors hacked one down and carted it home. Their souvenir was raised at Pioneer Place Park, where it remained until rot and an arsonist weakened it in 1938. Then the landmark was returned to Alaska, where Tlingit artists—remarkably unperturbed by Seattle's previous thievery—fashioned a replica.

Right: The Pioneer Building's one-story central tower was removed after Seattle's 1949 earthquake, lest it be toppled by a later temblor. Otherwise, the structure remains generally intact. It's now an office building but also serves as the starting point for the city's famous "underground tours," which take visitors beneath the streets of Pioneer Square.

Bank of Commerce Building

Located right across First Avenue from the Pioneer Building is the sandstone facade of the Bank of Commerce Building. Formerly called the Yesler Building because it was commissioned by Henry Yesler and raised in 1891 on the site of his original cookhouse, this structure is another legacy of Elmer H. Fisher. He designed the first three floors, but it was his draftsman, Emil DeNeuf, who is credited with adding the brick top story. Shortly after the building's completion, President Benjamin Harrison stepped onto its third-floor balcony in a heavy rain shower to thank Seattle's almost 43,000 residents—most of whom had shown up to watch—for their hospitality during his flag-waving tour of the Pacific Northwest.

Right: In honor of President Harrison's 1891 visit, a welcome arch—decorated with patriotic streamers and pine boughs—was raised on Yesler Way.

Above: A once-gilded 1889 menu from the Occidental Hotel

Occidental/Seattle Hotel

John Collins began life as a runaway from Ireland but ended it as "an entrepreneurial dynamo," to quote one columnist. Before being elected Seattle's fourth mayor in 1873, he made a fortune through investments in banking, railroading, gas lighting, real estate, streetcars, and other ventures. Confident of his adopted city's future, in 1884 Collins constructed what he boasted was "the leading hotel in the Northwest," the Occidental at the intersection of James Street and Yesler Way. Originally a brick, Second Empire–style building designed by Donald MacKay, the hotel operated only half a decade before succumbing to the 1889 blaze. Collins wasn't discouraged, insisting that "within a year we will have a city here that will surpass by far the town we had before the fire." He contributed to that dream by rebuilding his triangular hotel according to plans designed by MacKay's former draftsman, Stephen Meany. Collins died in 1903, but his inn (renamed the Seattle Hotel and shown at left, circa 1909) held on until 1963, when it was razed to make way for a 240-space parking structure, which is scornfully known as the "Sinking Ship" garage *(above)* due to its shape. Destruction of this hotel contributed to the birth of Seattle's preservation movement.

PIONEER SQUARE

Front Street (First Avenue) may be the oldest commercial thoroughfare in Pioneer Square, and it was certainly the most hectic when this neighborhood was still Seattle's business district. But Occidental Avenue South, one block to the east, used to be nearly as active. In the early 1900s, this roadway was lined with hotels, restaurants, and shops. An electric commuter train carried passengers from a terminal at Occidental and Yesler all the way south to downtown Tacoma. Like the rest of Pioneer Square, though, this road later suffered economic decline. Once the whole quarter became a historic district in 1970, trees were planted down the center of Occidental from Yesler Way to Jackson Street, and the two blocks between Jackson and Washington were closed to traffic. The street between Main and Jackson is now paved with red brick and hosts coffee shops and art galleries. One block north, from Washington to Main, is Occidental Park, a 0.6-acre square populated by totem poles carved by Duane Pasco. Occidental Park was originally paved with cobblestones salvaged from elsewhere in the neighborhood. However, a recent, controversial rehabilitation of the park replaced those stones with more even pavers, removed some overgrown trees, and added outdoor safety lighting. Artist Hai Ying Wu's Fallen Firefighters Memorial was installed in 1998.

Top: Occidental Avenue in the 1870s, looking north from Washington Street. *Bottom:* Occidental is no longer the busy place it once was, now catering to art gallery browsers and midday coffee drinkers.

Smith Tower

Lyman C. Smith was an inventor who, in the early 20th century, founded what would become the Smith-Corona Typewriter Company. Although his endeavors earned him recognition nationwide, in Seattle he is best remembered for constructing Smith Tower at James Street and Yesler Way—for many years the tallest skyscraper west of Ohio. As the story goes, Smith had originally planned a much shorter structure. However, his son, who believed Seattle had a great future, persuaded him to shoot for the sky. Smith hired Syracuse architects Edwin H. Gaggin and T. Walker Gaggin to create a Manhattan-style landmark. Smith Tower opened in 1914, four years after Smith's death. At 462 feet tall, it ruled Seattle's skyline until 1962, when the 605-foot Space Needle topped it. Its lobby is rich with marble, and on the 35th floor (right beneath the building's pyramidal cap) are an observation deck and the Chinese Room, noted for its carved wood and porcelain ceiling. The last manually operated elevators on the West Coast still run up and down Smith Tower. After passing through the hands of several owners, this beloved structure was purchased by a Chicago-based real-estate investment firm that has proposed converting 12 top floors into condominiums.

42 Story L.C. Smith Bldg.
SEATTLE

Above: A crowded cable car approaches the intersection of Yesler Way and Second Avenue, circa 1912.

In 1884, Seattle welcomed its first horse-drawn streetcar line, which ran along Second Avenue downtown. Just three years later, cable cars were introduced here, helping to tame the city's many steeper inclines. The original cable railway ran east on Yesler Way from Pioneer Square all the way to a park at Leschi on Lake Washington, returning along Jackson Street. Created by J. M. Thompson and local developer Fred Sander, the the Yesler cars encouraged the spread of cable lines to other parts of town, including up Front Street and over the top of Queen Anne Hill.

Left: The skeleton of Smith Tower, circa 1913

Katzenjammer Castle

The seat of local government has moved around more than a bit since Seattle was incorporated back in 1869. For a number of years, officials rented space, but in 1882 the first actual City Hall was established above a fire station in Pioneer Square. Unfortunately, that facility burned in 1889 along with the rest of downtown. In 1891, Mayor Harry White convinced the city to purchase a rickety-looking wooden structure on Third Avenue between Yesler Way and Jefferson Street, which had previously served as the King County Courthouse *(below)*. But almost immediately, the new building was determined to be inadequate. So additions were made—a basement courtroom was excavated, offices for the mayor and comptroller were tacked onto the south flank of the building, and new space was created for the city jail. Those add-ons, however, gave City Hall a ramshackle appearance and earned it the nickname "Katzenjammer Castle," because it resembled the chaotic architecture featured in a then-popular comic strip, *The Katzenjammer Kids*. Even before another year had passed, there were complaints of insufficient space. Finally, in 1909, Seattle's municipal government relocated again, to the then-new Yesler Building, a triangular, five-story edifice on the corner of Fifth Avenue and Yesler Way.

City Hall Park

Where Katzenjammer Castle once stood is now City Hall Park, a 1.3-acre, tree-shaded commons at Jefferson Street and Yesler Way, right next to the present-day King County Courthouse. The former City Hall and its adjacent structures were demolished when the courthouse (originally the City-County Building) was being constructed. That courthouse, seen on the right in this 1916 photo (with Smith Tower in the center and the Frye Hotel on the far left), was the work of architect Augustus Warren Gould. According to the book *Shaping Seattle Architecture: A Historical Guide to the Architects* (1994), Gould violated professional ethics to secure the courthouse commission. Anxious to erect a major work on that site, he openly sided with Pioneer Square property owners opposed to relocating city offices to the north end of downtown. For this breach, Gould was drummed out of the Washington state chapter of the American Institute of Architects. But he retained the courthouse project. His concept for the building (opened in 1916) called for a 22-story, H-shape skyscraper with a pyramid-topped tower rising from its center. Only five of the stories were completed before Gould's death in 1922. Six more were added by architect Henry Bittman in the early '30s, but the tower and Gould's other 11 floors never made it off the drawing board.

Left: A present-day look at the King County Courthouse

THE ORIGINAL WEST SEATTLE town site had been dubbed, with some hubris, "New York *Alki*," translated from the north-coast Chinook jargon as "New York by and by." Suquamish and Duwamish Indians called the area around Pioneer Square *Zechalalitch*, "the place to pass over," which didn't really suggest that it was a good place to stay. Yet the settlers who had moved east from Alki Point intended to do just that. They promptly named their new home on Elliott Bay, christening it "Duwamps." It was Doc Maynard's idea to give the promising hamlet a slightly more elegant moniker—one that honored an elderly leader of the local Suquamish, Chief Sealth *(right)*, or, as white tongues found it easier to pronounce, "Seattle."

Unfortunately, that tribute did little to improve still-uneasy relations between the white settlers and Northwest natives. On the morning of January 26, 1856, Indian raiders attacked the community, forcing residents to take shelter in a pair of log blockhouses and drawing cannon fire from the U.S. sloop-of-war *Decatur*, which had sailed into the area in anticipation of Indian hostilities. Two settlers were killed during this one-day "Battle of Seattle," along with an undetermined number of Native Americans.

GREAT FIRE OF 1889

Unlike San Francisco, which was already a metropolis when it burned in 1906, Seattle was still an overgrown small town on June 6, 1889, when it was struck by a devastating fire in the midst of a parched summer. The disaster actually began at the north end of today's Pioneer Square, in a cabinetmaker's basement shop at the corner of Front and Madison streets. Around 2:30 P.M., a pot of glue suddenly caught fire, and efforts to douse it with water only spread the flames into wood shavings on the floor. In just 30 minutes, the inferno was roaring south at a frightening clip, consuming whole blocks of Seattle's mainly wooden business district. Firefighters did what they could, but hydrant pressure was too low to stop the calamity's

progress. By 7 P.M., the fire had reached all the way to Main Street. Ironically, the city's fire chief was away in San Francisco at the time, attending a convention on advanced fire-fighting methodology. When it became obvious that his young acting chief was not up to this fight, Robert Moran, a shipyard owner who was then completing the first of his two single-year terms as Seattle's mayor, took command, ordering the demolition of buildings in front of the inferno and assembling 200-man bucket brigades to draw water from nearby gullies. Unfortunately, those efforts weren't enough. The conflagration was so violent, it raised an angry cloud of purplish smoke that was visible from Tacoma, 32 miles to the south.

Left: Looking south on Front Street (First Avenue) from Spring, about 30 minutes after the blaze began. Frye's Opera House is just catching fire.

Right: As the fire begins on Front Street near Madison, men struggle to extinguish it without success.

The Aftermath

Seattle's Great Fire of 1889 lasted for a frightening 12½ hours. By the time its violence was spent, 30 city blocks had been reduced to a stinking smudge on the Elliott Bay shore. Wharves were ruined, office buildings had collapsed, and chimneys protruded from broken lots like lonely survivors of a war. Everywhere, residents sifted through rubble, looking for pieces of their former lives. *Right:* Front Street (First Avenue), between Columbia and Yesler Way. *Below:* All that remained of the Yesler-Leary Building at Front and Yesler.

THE MAN WITH A PLAN

ALTHOUGH A NUMBER of architects helped rebuild Seattle after the Great Fire, the majority of large commissions went to a self-promoting Scottish immigrant named Elmer H. Fisher. More than anybody else, he established the look of what was then downtown Seattle and what is today Pioneer Square. Fisher's handsome creations in brick and stone, synthesizing Victorian design philosophies about facades with the popular but weighty Romanesque Revival look, soon decorated this city's skyline all the way from Jackson Street north to Belltown.

During the first two years after the fire, Fisher and his office full of draftsmen worked on more than 50 structures. Among the best known in Pioneer Square are the Pioneer Building and the Bank of Commerce Building, both at First and Yesler; the adjacent Schwabacher Building, which housed one of the city's first hardware stores; and his last major commission, the State Building, at Occidental and Main, finished in 1891. Sadly, many of Fisher's other edifices were demolished over the last century.

In 1893, at the height of his renown, Fisher was slapped with a breach of promise suit by an abandoned former mistress, who demanded $10,000 in damages. Although a jury eventually ruled that Fisher owed his former lover nothing, his reputation was destroyed. He disappeared from Seattle afterward and died in Los Angeles around 1905, a broken and seemingly forgotten man. However, history remembers him fondly as the man who re-created Seattle.

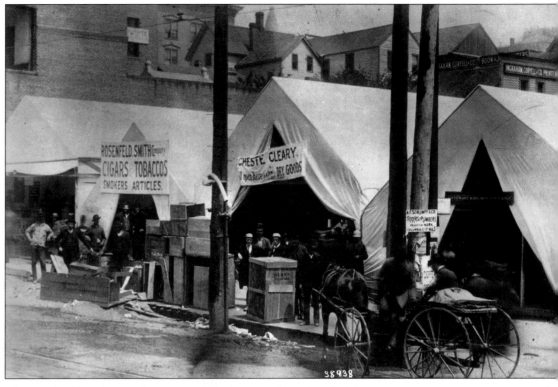

Above: Rebuilding along Yesler Way, with the Occidental Hotel on the left

Amazingly, not a single person is known to have died in the 1889 catastrophe. Even civic optimism seemed to come through without serious injury. With the rat-infested, sewage-bedeviled, and hurriedly constructed wooden town of old now flattened, civic boosters got busy reinventing Seattle, this time out of brick, stone, and iron. Streets would be widened and realigned, and new sewage and water systems installed. The first order of business was to lift the business district an entire story above its previous level. Tons of dirt from the town's eastern slopes were scraped down to fill the mudflats on which the original downtown had been constructed. In the meantime, new edifices were designed to accommodate the elevation change, with *two* sets of entrances: one at Seattle's original ground level, the other on the second story, where new streets and sidewalks would be laid. The problem was, the new raised streets went in well ahead of the sidewalks. So for a while, men and women crossing intersections had to scale ladders up one side of the street, then scurry over the raised pavement and climb down to the opposite sidewalk. When engineers finally built new sidewalks at the higher level, they didn't fill in beneath them, but instead left a subterranean network of original walkways and formal entrances. This "underground Seattle" is now a tourist attraction.

KLONDIKE GOLD RUSH

On the morning of July 17, 1897, the steamship *Portland* reached Seattle with 68 prospectors on board. They carried more than a ton of gold—riches panned from the frigid tributaries of the Klondike River in northwestern Canada's Yukon. It was the beginning of the famous Klondike Stampede, North America's last great frontier adventure. As the closest American rail-port to southeast Alaska, from which prospectors struggled up and over Chilkoot Pass to reach the gold fields around the Yukon's Dawson City, Seattle anticipated making a mint off this gold rush—and so it did. As many as 48 different mining firms opened offices in the Pioneer Building alone, and new hotels were raised just to catch the overflow from those that had existed before the rush began. During the first month of the stampede, up to 1,500 people shipped north from Seattle—including the mayor—with tens of thousands more to follow.

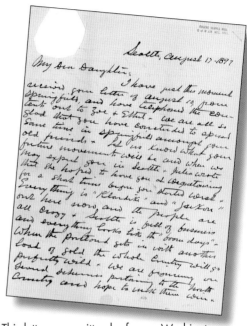

This letter was written by former Washington Territorial Governor Eugene Semple to his daughter in mid-August 1897, near the start of the gold rush. In it, he writes that "Everything is 'Klondike' and 'Yukon' out here now and the people are all crazy and Seattle is full of business and everything looks like the 'boom days' and when the *Portland* gets in with another load of gold the whole country will go perfectly wild…."

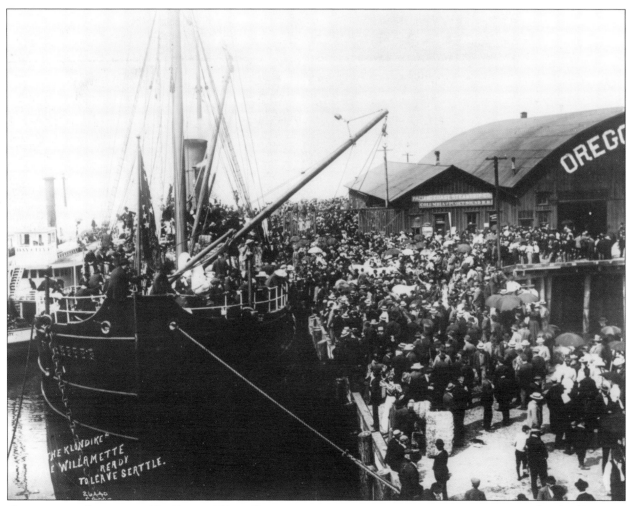

The steamer *Willamette* is mobbed by would-be millionaires on August 9, 1897, every one wanting to get to the Klondike pronto, even though many of them didn't really know where the Klondike was.

Stores such as Cooper & Levy on First Avenue (shown at right in 1897) ordered so many provisions for the Klondikers that piles of surplus were stacked up to ten feet high along sidewalks. Anything a gold seeker thought he needed could be bought in Seattle. Some people carried bicycles north with them, hoping to pedal their way to the precious metal. Others took dogsleds to be pulled by the packs of canines being imported into Seattle on a weekly basis. When actual sled dogs weren't available, fortune hunters just stole household pets. So many dogs were sent north from Seattle in 1897 and '98 that the city was proclaimed "a cat's paradise."

Most of the men (and fewer women) who set out for the Klondike had little understanding of the difficulties ahead. The usual route first took them up the Inside Passage—more than 1,000 miles from Seattle to southeastern Alaska. From there, they had to scale Chilkoot Pass (left, circa 1898) across the Coast Mountains and the Canadian border, a distance of 33 miles. Canada required that they pack along with them a year's worth of food and supplies—a burden that could weigh up to a ton and had to be transported in 50- or 60-pound portions over the pass. Once across the mountains into the Yukon, prospectors still had to travel another 550 miles through rough waterways to Dawson City. Despite these hardships, about 100,000 people joined the Klondike gold rush. Of those, maybe 4,000 actually found riches.

Union Depot, Seattle, Washington.

ALL ABOARD!

Talk of Seattle winning a transcontinental rail link was first heard in the early 1870s. Yet it wasn't until January 1893, after a couple of false starts and broken promises by the rival Northern Pacific Railroad, that James J. Hill's Great Northern Railway finally opened convenient access between Elliott Bay and the East Coast. But since the Great Northern arrived here amid a nationwide depression, there was little money or enthusiasm to mount a celebration. Seattle wouldn't really understand the benefits of rapid cross-country transportation until four years later, when gold seekers started flooding into this city on their way to Alaska and the Yukon.

Getting a railroad was one thing; getting a proper *railroad station* was another. In the 1890s, the Great Northern operated a scruffy depot on Marion Street. Seattleites impatient for a grander terminal were met with dismissive responses by Hill. Not until the early 20th century did Hill commission St. Paul, Minnesota, architects Charles Reed and Allen Stem, who had helped design New York City's Grand Central Station, to create an impressive depot (seen at left, circa 1911) on Jackson Street at the southern end of a $1.5-million, mile-long tunnel that Hill had excavated beneath downtown.

Hill's King Street Station opened in May 1906 and was originally the embarkation point for both the Great Northern and the Northern Pacific. Its brick-and-marble style is frequently referred to as "Railroad Italianate," and its most noticeable feature is a 120-foot clock tower, modeled after the campanile in Venice, Italy's, Piazza San Marco. Some of the terminal's interior spaces, though, were almost equally impressive. Its waiting room (right, circa 1906) was decorated with a coffered ceiling, chandeliers, and balconies. Unfortunately, during the 1950s and '60s, this structure's insides were "modernized," and much of the waiting room's plaster ornamentation was concealed behind a suspended acoustic tile ceiling. Only now is work under way to restore King Street Station (Seattle's Amtrak terminal) to its former grandeur.

Oregon & Washington Depot Seattle Wash.

Union Station

Not to be outshone, the Union Pacific Railroad, which finally reached the banks of Elliott Bay in 1910, raised its own imposing terminal just to the east of King Street Station. The architect was Daniel J. Patterson, who had worked as a draftsman for Seattle designer Willis Ritchie before relocating to San Francisco in the 1890s. His three-story, neoclassical train depot was completed in 1911 and would serve passengers for the next six decades, until Amtrak centralized this city's passenger-rail service at King Street Station. After sitting unused for many years, the monumental edifice, with its terra-cotta ornamentation and 55-foot-high vaulted Great Hall, was restored in the late 1990s as part of a larger development project. It now serves as the headquarters of Sound Transit.

1900 — April the 29th — 1900

HISTORY MADE!
THE PREMIER TRAIN OF THE
PIONEER NORTHWEST RAILWAY

The
NORTH COAST LIMITED
NORTHERN PACIFIC RAILWAY

NOW COMMENCING DAILY SERVICE
LINKING THE PROSPEROUS EAST WITH THE GOLDEN WEST
SEATTLE to ST. PAUL

And offering to the fastidious traveler
LUXURIOUS AND TASTEFUL ACCOMMODATIONS

THE NEW "ELECTRIC LIGHTS"
STEAM HEAT

Pullman's Palace Sleeping Cars

HIGHLY SCENIC ROUTE
FOLLOWING THE TRAIL OF LEWIS & CLARKE

Your Patronage Solicited!

Inset: A poster announcing the Northern Pacific Railway's introduction of its North Coast Limited train in 1900

INTERNATIONAL DISTRICT

Many of the first Chinese to reach Puget Sound had originally been drawn to the West Coast by the California Gold Rush of the late 1840s or by construction of the First Transcontinental Railroad in the 1860s. They eventually drifted north to find employment in sawmills, laundries, mines, restaurants, and canneries. By the 1870s, a small Chinatown had blossomed along Washington Street, in what is now Pioneer Square. For at least a decade, whites, Chinese, and Japanese (who began arriving there in the late '70s) coexisted peacefully. But by the mid-1880s, economic downturns and Seattle's inability to secure transcontinental rail connections convinced many laborers to leave. Those who stayed frequently blamed their idleness on cheaper Chinese workers, who were supposedly *stealing* their jobs. "The Chinese must go!" became an all-too-familiar rallying cry—one that only intensified after passage of the Chinese Exclusion Act of 1882, forbidding further Chinese immigration to the United States and denying citizenship rights to those already settled here. Job frustrations eventually boiled over into violence. In September 1885, three Chinese hop-pickers were shot to death while they slept in their tents in what's now Issaquah, east of Seattle. Two months later, a Tacoma mob descended upon that town's Asian quarter, forcing some 200 inhabitants onto a train headed south for Portland, Oregon. Then, in February 1886, throngs of Seattle xenophobes (including, it's said, many police officers) invaded Chinatown and herded almost all of its 350 to 400 occupants toward steamships bound for San Francisco. Martial law was declared to halt this expulsion, and U.S. President Grover Cleveland sent federal troops to Seattle to maintain order. But at least half of the Chinese wound up leaving the city anyway, fearful of the consequences should they stay.

Left: An 1886 illustration from *Harper's Weekly* depicts the violence of the anti-Chinese riots in Seattle.

Filling the vacuum—and many of the jobs—left behind by the Chinese were Japanese newcomers. Though not specifically affected by the Exclusion Act, they were prevented by law from becoming American citizens, owning land, and even renting homes in some Seattle neighborhoods (such as West Seattle and Magnolia). They were also fresh targets of racism. However, the Japanese continued to arrive here in increasing numbers, gathering together into a vibrant community known as Japantown, or Nihonmachi, at the southern end of downtown, on land reclaimed from formerly fetid tide flats. By 1910, Nihonmachi—with its restaurants, hotels, public baths, and gambling dens (which drew white patrons, as well)—housed more than 6,000 Japanese. *Left:* The Yamatoya dry-goods store on Jackson Street, circa 1910.

Above: Today, Jackson Street provides easy access between the International District and Pioneer Square, inviting downtown office workers to take their lunches at one of the International District's many restaurants.

Not long after the 1889 fire destroyed the Asian community along with the rest of Pioneer Square, Chinese residents who remained here began rebuilding. This time, though, they didn't put up one-story, wood-frame buildings on the margins of downtown; instead, they raised impressive brick structures of several stories around the intersection of Second Avenue South and South Washington Street. They built hotels for travelers arriving at Seattle's brand-new train stations. And they carried on traditions that made their continuing presence known. The photograph above shows a Chinese dragon parade along Third Avenue South in 1900. Chinatown persisted until the late 1920s, when Second Avenue was extended south from Yesler Way and much of that neighborhood was razed. Its residents relocated to Nihonmachi, where they joined a complex ethnic mix that also included Filipinos, who had been relocating to Seattle ever since the Spanish-American War of 1898.

Chong Wa Benevolent Association

Established around 1915 to advocate Chinese American rights in Washington, the Chong Wa Benevolent Association has occupied this two-story brick structure on Seventh Avenue South and South Weller Street since 1929. Designed by Max Van House and Sam Wing Chin (the latter being the state's first Asian American graduate in architecture, in 1922), it blends Western forms with Chinese motifs. The benevolent association now operates a Chinese language school and offers citizenship classes. *Above:* A group poses in front of the Chong Wa building in 1930.

Wartime Internments

By the start of World War II, Japanese Americans made up Seattle's largest ethnic minority. But in the wake of Japan's attack on Pearl Harbor, Hawaii, in December 1941, even Japanese-descended Seattleites who'd never so much as visited the land of their ancestors were tarred as "the enemy." (*Below:* An anti-Japanese window display at the downtown Frederick and Nelson department store in 1943.) Two months after the attack, more than 12,000 Japanese American Washingtonians—including 7,000 from Seattle—were sent to inland internment camps, most of those from the Puget Sound area going to southern Idaho's Minidoka Relocation Center. As time passed, restrictions were relaxed, and in January 1943, the U.S. military even began admitting Nisei (second-generation Japanese Americans). However, it wasn't until the war's end in 1945 that the Japanese were allowed to return to Seattle. They found a much-changed community. A rundown section of the neighborhood had been demolished to make room for Yesler Terrace, an integrated public-housing project that housed some of the thousands of African Americans who had come to Seattle looking for wartime employment with Boeing. And legislation introduced by then U.S. Representative Warren G. Magnuson of Washington had overturned the Chinese Exclusion Act in 1943, allowing a greater influx of immigrants from all over Asia.

Wing Luke

Even two decades after the Exclusion Act's repeal, Asian Americans remained largely segregated south of Yesler Way. But in March 1962, businessman and civic activist Wing Luke won a seat on the Seattle City Council, becoming the first Chinese American elected to a major post in the continental United States. Luke gave Chinese Americans a higher profile in this city, but he also earned broader favor by championing civil rights, historic preservation, and an end to racial discrimination in housing. Had Luke not died in a small-plane crash in the Cascade Mountains in May 1965, he may have gone on to much higher political office. His memory is kept green by the Wing Luke Asian Museum, an excellent facility on South King Street. *Left:* Wing Luke speaking to the Women's Traffic and Transportation Club in Seattle, 1964.

An Evolving Community

In recognition of the neighborhood's increasing ethnic diversity, Seattle Mayor William F. Devin decreed in 1951 that it be dubbed "International Center." Opponents argued that this would diminish public recognition of both Chinese and Japanese historical influences on the area. But greater threats were posed by the demolition of older Asian-owned buildings, construction in the early 1960s of Interstate 5 (which cut straight through the district's heart), and the building in the 1970s of the Kingdome sports arena, which brought traffic congestion to the quarter. Fortunately, during the late 20th century, as this melting-pot precinct was further enriched by Korean, Vietnamese, Laotian, and Cambodian immigrants, revitalization efforts were made. In 1987, the neighborhood was awarded federal protection as the "Seattle Chinatown Historic District." Eleven years later, it became the "Chinatown/International District"—a hybrid moniker that still generates debate. Once-dilapidated hotels have since been converted into low-income housing; Uwajimaya Village, a retail-residential complex on Fifth Avenue South, draws Seattleites in search of high-quality Chinese foodstuffs; and Hing Hay Park *(right)*, a quarter-block open space that includes a colorful Chinese pavilion (a gift from the people of Taipei, Taiwan) and a huge dragon mural, has become a major focal point for community celebrations, including Chinese New Year and the International District Summer Festival.

INDIAN CAMP SEATTLE, WASH.

WATERFRONT

The pioneers who relocated here from West Seattle in the early 1850s found a natural shoreline at what's now more or less First Avenue South, along with a small area of flat land that is occupied by today's Pioneer Square. To the north and east were forested hill slopes. Marshland could be found south of Yesler Way and north of South King Street. Still farther south were tide flats that practically challenged anyone to build atop them.

From Yesler's Wharf (constructed in 1853 but later expanded), sailing ships carried local lumber to California. Additional docks sprouted along the shoreline like jagged teeth, handling coal and grain shipments. In 1882,

giant Colman Dock began welcoming cross-Sound passenger vessels, and the waterfront became a bustling transportation zone. As late as the early 1890s, Native Americans (mostly Duwamish) who had been driven out of town returned every September to work in the hop fields southeast of Seattle. They tethered their dugouts and camped at what was known as "Ballast Island" (shown at left, circa 1891), a dismal patch of land created from dumped ships' ballasts at the foot of Washington Street (where the Washington Street Public Boat Landing now stands). White settlers crowded around to see these "exotic" interlopers and maybe buy the baskets they brought to sell or barter for other goods.

FROM THE ODD TO THE OUTRAGEOUS

Part *Ripley's Believe It or Not*, part showman P. T. Barnum's back room, Ye Olde Curiosity Shop (pictured at right, circa 1908) is unlike anything else in the city. It was founded in 1899 by Joseph E. "Daddy" Standley, an Ohio-born curio collector. The store was originally housed at Second Avenue and Pike Street but moved to Madison Street in 1901 and to Colman Dock on Pier 52 in 1904. Standley stocked Aleut grass baskets, seal-fur moccasins, ivory trinkets, and thousands of miniature totem poles, as well as Indian goods imported from the Plains states and the Southwest. Displayed prominently among those wares were a plethora of not-for-sale oddities, including the Lord's Prayer printed on the head of a pin, shrunken heads, and an alleged mermaid. Massive whale bones were displayed out front. Although Standley died in 1940, the store carried on. Current "attractions" include a bottled pig with eight legs and "Sylvester," a mummified murder victim found in 1895. The shop is currently located at Pier 54.

Railroad Ave. Seattle

As the 19th century slid into the 20th, Seattle's waterfront piers were rebuilt to accommodate an increasing sea trade with Asia. While the waterfront brought commercial prosperity to the city, it wasn't easily accessible to pedestrians. Behind the piers stretched Railroad Avenue (shown above, circa 1898), so named because it had been dominated since 1874 by steel tracks atop wooden planks and trestles. Pedestrians had to cross at one of three overpasses located at Bell, Pike, and Marion streets. In 1911, voters created a Port of Seattle district that eventually wrested control of the waterfront from railway interests. Construction of a seawall and sidewalk along the Sound began in 1916, and the process of dirt-filling the area previously occupied by Railroad Avenue created the land over which Alaskan Way now runs. During the 1950s, the city constructed the Alaskan Way Viaduct, an elevated, double-deck, reinforced-concrete section of State Route 99 that overshadows the waterfront. Many people now decry the viaduct as ugly and—in the event of a serious earthquake—dangerous. However, there remains no consensus on whether it should be razed, rebuilt, or replaced with something else.

Ivar Haglund established Seattle's first aquarium at Pier 54 in 1938. After watching a friend's fish-and-chips stand fail at the aquarium, Haglund created his own seafood eatery, Ivar's Acres of Clams, in 1946. The aquarium closed ten years later, but the restaurant at Pier 54 (*below*) is still going strong. A self-effacing folk musician, Ivar promoted his eatery with pun-filled jingles he sang on the radio. He also sponsored comical clam-eating contests. However, he may be best remembered for the slogan "Keep Clam," which still adorns the Ivar's seafood chain. This "unofficial mayor of the waterfront" died in January 1985, but his love of amusements lives on in the annual Ivar's Fourth of July fireworks blowout over Elliott Bay.

FERRIES

The first steamship to make regular runs between Seattle and other Puget Sound communities was the *Eliza Anderson*, a side-wheeler that began service here in 1859. Its temporary transportation monopoly was noted by one wag, who said, "No steamer went so slow or made money faster." Over the next decade, the number of cross-Sound vessels expanded substantially, their often modest size and ubiquity recognized in their collective nickname, "the Mosquito Fleet." In 1882, businessman James M. Colman finally built a dock for these passenger-only craft at the foot of Columbia Street (*below*)—the precursor to today's Washington State Ferry Terminal at Colman Dock. Christmas Eve, 1888, saw the launching of this city's first regularly scheduled ferry service, carrying passengers aboard the side-wheeler *City of Seattle* from downtown to Duwamish Head in West Seattle. A second ferry, the *West Seattle*, made its debut 19 years later. The Mosquito Fleet's heyday continued from the 1880s to the 1920s and involved some 2,500 ships. But following the construction of San Francisco's Golden Gate Bridge and Bay Bridge in the 1930s, a variety of out-of-work diesel-electric automobile ferries were brought north to replace the Mosquito flotilla. The last of those privately owned vessels disappeared in the mid-20th century, when the state of Washington assumed public control over cross-Sound ferry service.

121 MOTOR FERRY "KALAKALA", WORLD'S FIRST STREAMLINED VESSEL

IN SERVICE BETWEEN SEATTLE AND BREMERTON, WASH. ON PUGET SOUND

When the silver-skinned, aerodynamically designed *Kalakala* (shown at left, circa 1946) was launched on Puget Sound in 1935, it was considered the height of 20th-century progress. Built atop the iron hull of a San Francisco ferry that had burned to her waterline two years earlier, the *Kalakala* was the largest and swiftest ferry on the Sound at the time, carrying up to 2,000 passengers and 100 automobiles per trip between Seattle and Bremerton. It boasted a double-horseshoe lunch counter, three large observation rooms, and 500 velvet-upholstered easy chairs. The vessel even had its own eight-piece orchestra, its music piped throughout the ship for evening dancing. Although it was notorious for its noise, vibration, and minor collisions (with both docks and other ships), the *Kalakala* was a much-photographed attraction. However, as cars grew larger and harder to squeeze in and as foot passengers fell in number, the *Kalakala* became too expensive to operate. It was finally auctioned off in 1967 and spent the next 31 years as a fish processor in Alaska. The *Kalakala* returned to Seattle in 1998, but after several failed preservation attempts, the ship was removed to Tacoma, where it awaits restoration.

While Puget Sound was being stitched thickly with shipping routes, mammoth Lake Washington, on the city's east side, gave rise to similar enterprises. The first steamships appeared on that waterway in the 1870s, and by the mid-1880s, craft such as the *Squak* and the *Hattie Hansen* began transporting cargo and passengers from Seattle to Meydenbauer Bay, at what's now Bellevue. In the 1890s, Seattleites could take day trips across Lake Washington to visit the elegant Hotel Calkins on Mercer Island or sail to the would-be industrial capital of Kirkland for business or pleasure. Steamers such as the *L. T. Haas* (shown at left, circa 1911) and the *Cyrene*, along with the ferries *Issaquah* and *Leschi* (the latter being the first to carry cars over the lake, beginning in 1913), did a brisk business in cross-lake travel until interurban trains and automobiles became commonplace in the early 20th century. The lake's last ferry, the *Leschi*, stopped running in 1950, a decade after the opening of the first Lake Washington floating bridge.

FINANCIAL DISTRICT

Scottish-born master mechanic James M. Colman operated sawmills on the western banks of Puget Sound before arriving in Seattle in 1872. Backed by San Francisco financiers, Colman leased Yesler's Mill in Pioneer Square. He later constructed the Seattle & Walla Walla Railroad, which linked this city with the Newcastle coal mines to the southeast. Shortly before the Great Fire of 1889, Colman engaged architect Stephen Meany to create a five-story classical revival office building on Front Street (First Avenue) between Marion and Columbia streets. Work on it had barely begun before downtown was wiped out. In 1890, Colman built the first two levels of his new commercial block but then stopped, testing the market before he continued. Work on the edifice didn't resume until 1904—this time under the supervision of Norwegian-born architect August Tidemand. The original structure was retained but radically revamped, and four more brick-faced stories were added, the whole taking on a Chicago-school look, as seen in the 1909 photo *(top)*. A 1929 remodel by architect Arthur B. Loveless added a glass sidewalk canopy and other art deco trimmings.

Right: Today's First Avenue, looking north from Marion Street. On the left is the brick and terra-cotta old Federal Office Building (1933).

New York Block

William Boone was considered to be Seattle's finest architect prior to the 1889 fire, and he continued to practice here until 1910. Sadly, most of his works have since been demolished (with the notable exception of the 1891 Globe Building at South Main Street and First Avenue South in Pioneer Square, now home to the Elliott Bay Book Company). One of the most missed is Boone's magnificent 1892 New York Block (pictured below, circa 1920), which sat on the northeast corner of Second Avenue and Cherry Street. Unlike the Victorian edifices for which Boone was originally known, this seven-story pile of brick and rusticated stone displayed the influences of Boston architect Henry Hobson Richardson. Not long after that, the New York Block was torn down to make room for the E-shape, terra-cotta-clad Dexter Horton Building, which was completed in 1924 according to plans by architect John Graham, Sr. The Dexter Horton Building still stands today.

Women risked their flowered hats—not to mention their lives—by leaning out over the top of the six-story Bailey Building (now known as the Broderick Building) at Cherry Street and Second Avenue in 1908 *(above)*. Like others on the floors below, they watched a naval parade, likely the one held in May of that year to welcome "the Great White Fleet" to Puget Sound. Comprising 16 white-painted battleships and some 4,000 sailors, that flotilla took 14 months to circumnavigate the globe in a show of U.S. naval supremacy engineered by outgoing President Theodore Roosevelt.

First Avenue

Seattle's northward expansion at the turn of the last century was most evident along First Avenue (previously Front Street). What had once been narrow, uneven boardwalks plumped into broad concrete sidewalks trod by the powerful as well as the destitute. Where buildings had once been squat and few in number, they suddenly reached for the clouds in a hectic canyon of commercialism shaped from brick and terra-cotta. And everywhere, it seemed, there were streetcars and wagons, horse-drawn cabs, and, eventually, early automobiles. The photo at left shows First Avenue looking north from Cherry Street in 1911. Elmer H. Fisher's now long-gone Sullivan Building (1891), a composite of classical and Romanesque motifs, dominates the near-right corner of this image.

Burke Building

Completed in 1891, the Burke Building (above, circa 1905) at Second Avenue and Marion Street was considered one of Seattle's finest business blocks. Its designer was Elmer H. Fisher, who had helped establish the architectural vernacular of postfire Pioneer Square. The client was Thomas Burke, lawyer, railroad builder, and chief justice of the Supreme Court of the Washington Territory. Burke suggested that Fisher look to the work of Chicago architects Daniel Burnham and John Wellborn Root—specifically their famous 1888 Rookery Building in the Chicago Loop—for inspiration. Fisher's response was to create a six-story Richardsonian Romanesque structure of stone and brick, replete with arches and an elegant variety of columns, with a corner of curved masonry and glass. That edifice stood until 1973, when—despite protests from architects and preservationists—it was torn down and replaced by the much less interesting Henry M. Jackson Federal Office Building. *Right:* The Burke Building's arched Second Avenue entranceway and other of its decorative features were incorporated into a plaza outside the new Federal Office Building's tower.

Princess Angeline

The oldest daughter of Native American leader Chief Sealth, Princess Angeline was born around 1810. She was originally known as Kikisoblu (or Kickisomlo) but was rechristened Angeline by Catherine Maynard, Doc Maynard's second wife, who insisted: "You are far too handsome to carry a name like that." Angeline lived for many years in a crude cedar shack to the west of today's Pike Place Market and eschewed the efforts of "benevolent ladies" to find her more comfortable digs. She was frequently spotted on Seattle's downtown streets and was often the target of visiting photographers. After Angeline died in 1896, she was buried in Lake View Cemetery on Capitol Hill near her friend, pioneer Henry Yesler.

Seattle Tower

Often called this city's finest art deco skyscraper, the Seattle Tower (originally the Northern Life Tower) was completed in 1929 and is credited to the local architectural firm Albertson, Wilson & Richardson. The principal designer was reportedly Illinois-born Joseph Wilson, who had come to Washington in 1907 in search of his brother, a timber cruiser who'd disappeared here. The Northern Life Insurance Company wanted a Puget Sound headquarters that symbolized permanence and dependability; what they got was a mountain. The tower, shown at left in 1929, is tapered to emphasize its verticality. The exterior brickwork becomes lighter the farther up it goes. Piers are mantled with lighter terra-cotta to suggest snow-capped peaks. The mountain motif is continued inside, where a great ornamented lobby suggests a tunnel carved through an alpine slope.

Potlatch

Conceived both as a celebration of the prosperity Seattle had enjoyed since the Klondike Gold Rush and an opportunity to tout the town's regional dominance, the Potlatch festival was held here annually beginning in 1911. It traded on the North Coast Native American concept of *potlatch*, defined as a "carnival of sports, music, dancing and feasting, and the distributing of gifts by the hosts to all the guests." Parades were held, with local dignitaries crowded onto canoe-shape floats and others marching in totem pole costumes (right, circa 1912). The initial Potlatch featured automobile races up Queen Anne Hill and a reenactment of the first gold-bearing ship arriving at Seattle from Alaska in 1897. Everything went smoothly until 1913, when politics infringed on the festival, provoking a riot between servicemen and supposedly socialist members of the Industrial Workers of the World union. The 1914 Potlatch was the last one until 1934, when organizers revived the event as a tonic for spirits brought low by the Great Depression. The last Potlatch was held in 1941. Nine years later, the nautical-themed Seafair took its place as Seattle's summertime celebration.

HOTELS

Most of Seattle's early hotels were built in what's now Pioneer Square. But after the Great Fire of 1889, a group of "public spirited capitalists," including Judge Thomas Burke, raised a grand new inn north of the burn zone. The fortresslike Rainier Hotel (shown below in 1891) was built almost entirely of wood and occupied the hilltop block between Columbia and Marion streets and Fifth and Sixth avenues. Designed by Bostonian Charles W. Saunders (later responsible for the University of Washington's chateauesque Denny Hall) and Brit Edwin W. Houghton, the Rainier

Hotel was constructed in a mere 80 days to accommodate people left homeless by the fire or those visiting Seattle to help with its resurrection. Guests were treated to gasp-inspiring views of the Sound from the hotel's wraparound veranda, as well as a clear outlook on the King County Courthouse (visible on the distant right). But, as Pioneer Square's brick hostelries reopened, fewer and fewer overfed Victorians made the steep climb to this timber castle. The Rainier lost $100,000 in five years and was turned into an apartment structure before being torn down in the early 20th century.

Olympic Hotel

Not until after World War I did Seattle start agitating for the construction of a hotel to reflect its big-city aspirations. After going several rounds with the University of Washington Board of Regents, who still controlled the retail shopping district's "Metropolitan Tract," a deal was finally reached to raise a monumental inn on the block bounded by Fourth and Fifth avenues and University and Seneca streets. A public campaign sold $3 million worth of bonds, and New York architect George B. Post (who'd worked on the 1893 Chicago World's Fair and created the Wisconsin Capitol) was hired to design the building, along with locals Charles F. Gould and Charles H. Bebb. In 1924, their giant new Italian palazzo-style Olympic Hotel (named after a local business leader's yacht) opened amid newspaper hoopla. Sixty years later, the Seattle architectural firm NBBJ renovated the property, reducing the number of guest rooms in order to enlarge them, and creating a more impressive main entrance on Seneca. The Olympic (shown here in 1929) is now managed by Fairmont Hotels & Resorts of Canada.

Westin Hotel

Rising 40 stories above the Denny Regrade area, what was originally known as the Washington Plaza Hotel—today's Westin Hotel—was the work of architect John Graham, Jr., who had previously created the Space Needle. The first of its two towers (above, circa 1969) was completed in 1969, with a second, slightly taller twin going up in 1982 (shown at right). Because of its shape, Seattleites often direct visitors to the Westin by saying "look for the corncob towers."

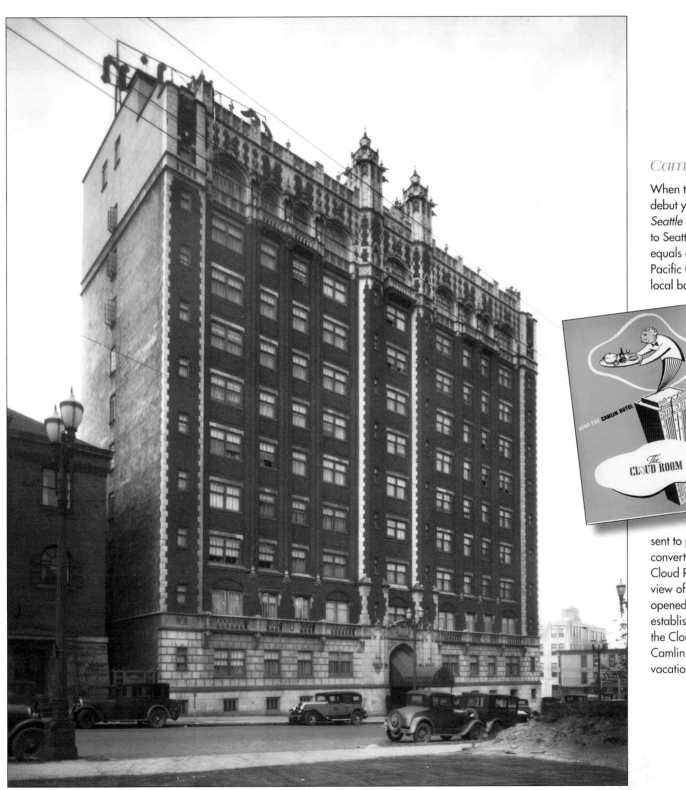

Camlin Hotel

When the Camlin Hotel (shown at left in its debut year) opened on Halloween in 1926, *The Seattle Times* said "it stands as a monument to Seattle's development, a mark which equals anything to be found anywhere on the Pacific Coast." Financed by two ambitious local bankers, Adolph Linden and Edmund Campbell, this 11-story inn at Ninth Avenue and Pine Street was designed by Carl J. Linde, a one-time brewery architect from Portland, Oregon. The basic style was Gothic, complete with lions' heads and decorative gargoyles. Though impressive, the project was soon scandalized, as news came out that Linden and Campbell had embezzled the funds to build the Camlin from their bank. Both men were subsequently prosecuted and sent to prison. In 1947, the hotel's then owners converted a penthouse suite into the legendary Cloud Room, a restaurant with a 360-degree view of downtown. Until the Space Needle opened in 1962, the city offered no dining establishment closer to the stars. Unfortunately, the Cloud Room was closed in 2003, and the Camlin has since been converted into a private vacation resort. *Inset:* A Cloud Room menu.

LIBRARIES

Today, Seattle is known as one of the most literate cities in America. But it wasn't until half a century after its founding that the town finally established a permanent home for its lending library. In 1868, some 50 residents got together to create a library association, appointing Sarah Yesler, the wife of industrialist and real-estate mogul Henry Yesler, as the first librarian. Mrs. Yesler was an advocate of women's suffrage and a spiritualist who believed in free love (a good thing, since by the time she reached Puget Sound, Henry had sired a daughter with a Native American mistress). She was also instrumental in starting the town's collection of books, most of which came from Boston. In 1891, four years after Sarah Yesler's demise,

Seattle's first public reading room opened on the fifth floor of the Occidental Hotel in Pioneer Square. At that point, the library's holdings comprised 7,000 books and 180 periodicals. However, as the collection grew, the library moved several times, eventually settling in 1899 in Henry and Sarah Yesler's mansion, at the intersection of Third Avenue and James Street (shown below, circa 1899), the present site of the King County Courthouse. Henry had left that Victorian residence to the city upon his death in 1892. The collection's future seemed assured—until a fire in 1901 destroyed the Yesler Mansion, taking 25,000 books with it.

East Coast industrialist and philanthropist Andrew Carnegie was approached prior to the Yesler Mansion blaze by Seattleites hoping he would finance construction of a grander public book repository. He refused, insisting that Seattle was little more than a "hot air boom town." After the fire, though, Carnegie agreed to contribute $200,000 toward a new library, provided the city supply a site (the block bounded by Fourth and Fifth avenues and Madison and Spring streets) as well as an annual maintenance budget of $50,000. Chicago architect Peter J. Weber designed the new edifice, a broad-shouldered masonry Beaux Arts–style landmark that opened in 1906 (shown below, circa 1956). Fronted by gargantuan pillars and an imposing staircase (added to the building after regrading lowered Fourth Avenue by ten feet), the 55,000-square-foot Central Library offered voluminous interior spaces, including an elegant main reading room (inset, circa 1906). The 1949 earthquake damaged Carnegie's palace of books, but it was not until 1957 that the structure was leveled and an international-style substitute was raised on the same steep site.

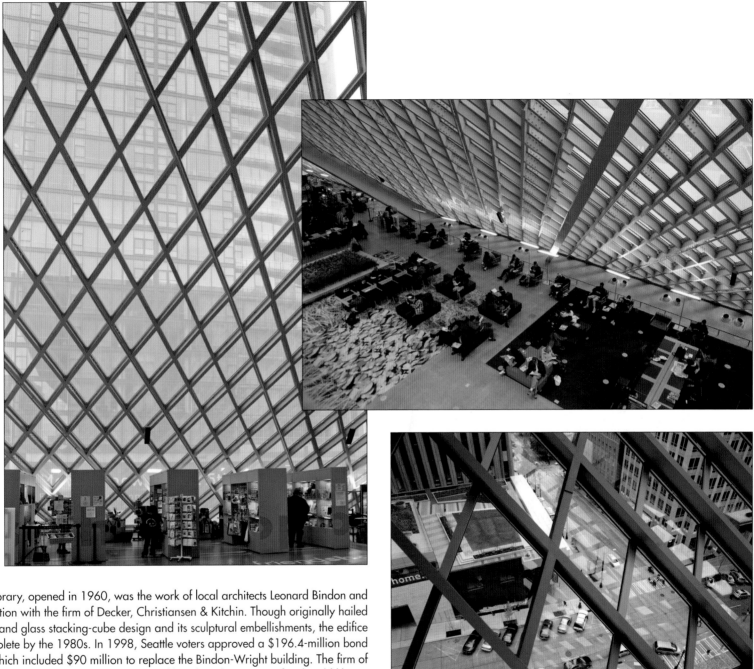

The city's third Central Library, opened in 1960, was the work of local architects Leonard Bindon and John L. Wright in association with the firm of Decker, Christiansen & Kitchin. Though originally hailed for its Modernist granite and glass stacking-cube design and its sculptural embellishments, the edifice was considered obsolete by the 1980s. In 1998, Seattle voters approved a $196.4-million bond issue for libraries, which included $90 million to replace the Bindon-Wright building. The firm of Dutch designer Rem Koolhaas received the commission, and less than three years after the old library collapsed before a wrecking ball, Seattle's latest and much-praised Central Library *(left)* opened its doors. It's an asymmetrical, cantilevered eye-catcher of steel and glass, filled with high-tech resources and offering stunning views of Elliott Bay and Mount Rainier.

PIKE PLACE MARKET

Seattle's historic downtown bazaar—the oldest continuously operating farmers market in the country—was born out of protest. In the early 1900s, some 3,000 farms supplied city residents with their fresh vegetables and fruits. But growers griped that the food wholesalers along Western Avenue, who bought their goods and then sold them to consumers, were profiting too much on both ends. So, with encouragement from recently elected city council member Thomas P. Revelle, they organized a public market along a plank-covered stretch of Pike Place, just west of First Avenue. Fewer than a dozen produce wagons appeared on the market's opening day, August 17, 1907, but hundreds of Seattleites came to strip those wagons bare. The next week, six dozen wagons arrived and were also emptied within hours. By November, real-estate developer Frank Goodwin had raised the first permanent commercial building on the site, and within ten years most of the structures that now make up the Market were in place. The original mix of produce sellers soon grew to include fishmongers, butter and cheese peddlers, candy makers, butchers operating from behind curtains of hanging chickens, and myriad producers of handmade crafts. Pike Place Market had become a robust, rambling hive of capitalism. *Below, left:* The corner of Pike and First Avenue in 1910. The billboards seen here were replaced by the Corner Market Building.

Above: Today, visitors to Pike Place Market will find Rachel, a piggy bank whose funds go to the Market Foundation. Rachel was added to the market in 1986.

The Klondike Gold Rush of 1897–1899, followed immediately by the rush for riches on the beaches of Nome, Alaska, flushed thousands of avaricious prospectors through Seattle. It also created commercial links between this city and the District of Alaska (later the Alaska Territory). Furs, native-made trinkets, and wild game were soon being shipped south for sale. At this Alaska Deer Market on Pike Place *(right)*, venison steaks, roasts, and sausages could be purchased, and free samples were cut for passersby who had not yet tried the Last Frontier's most common comestible.

Frank Goodwin's Main Arcade *(left)* now contains about half of the Market's fish and produce stalls. Rising over the arcade is the Public Market Center sign with its prominent clock—reportedly the oldest example of public neon in Seattle, dating to the 1920s or '30s.

Something for Every Table

Almost anything a family needed for its pantry could be had among Pike Place Market's stalls and storefronts. The Waterfront Fish and Oyster Company (top, circa 1914) drew on the abundance of seafood available from both Puget Sound and the city's surrounding rivers. Cooks came here to look over the fresh farm goods available from sellers such as the Valley Vegetable Gardens (bottom left, circa 1928). And everywhere there were Europeans, Asians, and even Sephardic Jews hawking their wares. Children brought north from an orphanage in Des Moines gave concerts on the sidewalks; off-duty maids lingered over hot chocolate at cafés; and old-timers wove twine into sturdy shopping bags while recalling their Klondike adventure days. The Great Depression later took a toll on this place, though, as did the World War II-era internment of Japanese, who operated a majority of the farms around Seattle.

Saving the Market

After World War II, there was a significant decline in the number of farmer-vendors at Pike Place Market. In 1953, the double-decked Alaskan Way Viaduct cut that commercial complex off from the waterfront, and nearby First Avenue's slow but steady transformation into a honky-tonk strip scared people away from the area. The *Seattle Post-Intelligencer* finally proposed alleviating downtown's worsening parking problems by demolishing the Market in favor of a seven-story garage. Others wanted to fill the site with a new hotel and office towers. In 1963, the city council voted to tear down all but a small portion of Pike Place Market. Fortunately, a preservation campaign was quickly mounted, sparked by council member Wing Luke and led in part by local architect Victor Steinbrueck and renowned painter Mark Tobey. Protestors took to the streets (below, 1971), and walking tours of the Market helped remind Seattleites what they were in danger of losing. Although the cards seemed stacked against the Market's survival, a 1971 ballot initiative won overwhelming voter support, creating a seven-acre historic district. The city went on to invest more than $50 million, including funds received from federal grants, to restore the Market. Today it is one of Seattle's most prized institutions, though critics sometimes object to its growing role as a tourist draw rather than a venue for grocery shopping.

The Original Starbucks

When the first Starbucks Coffee store opened at Pike Place Market in 1971, nobody could have known how that enterprise would change the morning drinking habits of people worldwide. Named after either Mr. Starbuck, the java-junkie first mate in Herman Melville's *Moby Dick*, or an old mining camp (Starbo) on Mount Rainier, Starbucks started out roasting and wholesaling beans for folks who craved a more flavorful cup of joe. But in 1984, at the suggestion of Howard Schultz, the company's director of marketing, Starbucks opened its first espresso bar at Fourth Avenue and Spring Street. Seattleites were quickly seduced by the heady aromas and richer tastes—not to mention the arcane ordering lingo—of espresso, and by the early 1990s, local columnists already referred to Seattle as "Lattéland." Today, Starbucks operates in 43 countries outside the United States. Schultz serves as the company's chairman and CEO, and the original corporate logo—showing a bare-breasted, twin-tailed siren-mermaid—has been stylized to be, well, somewhat less revealing. But that first Starbucks outlet at 1912 Pike Place *(top)* is still going strong. *Bottom:* Even before Starbucks opened, the Market did a brisk business in beans at the Filipino Coffee Company (shown circa 1909) and elsewhere.

SHOPPING DISTRICT

The University of Washington got its start at Fourth Avenue and University Street, where the Fairmont Olympic Hotel now stands. Not long after the Territorial Legislature gave its blessing to Seattle as the home of a university in 1861, pioneer Arthur Denny offered ten acres of his property on a thickly forested knoll above the town as an appropriate spot on which to build it. Quickly, a main Territorial University building, a boardinghouse, and a president's residence were built. Yesler's Mill supplied most of the lumber, while brick came south from Bellingham, Washington, and glass and hardware were imported from the Canadian island town of Victoria, British Columbia. The completed university opened on November 4, 1861, with 30 students. Not until 1895 did it move to its present location on Portage Bay, northeast of Lake Union. The photograph below (circa 1880) shows the north side of the original campus's main structure, with the steeple of old Plymouth Congregational Church on the right.

Seattle streets welcomed their first automobile in 1900. By 1940, when the picture above was taken, there were enough local roadway fatalities to warrant publicizing them with a "traffic death thermometer" at Fourth Avenue and Pike Street. A high school band, Red Cross representatives, and city officials helped draw attention to the hazards.

Cobb and White-Henry-Stuart Buildings

A year before the original Territorial University building was demolished in 1908, a master plan for developing the ten-acre downtown university site was prepared by New York architects John Mead Howells and I. N. Phelps Stokes, along with Seattle designer Abraham Albertson. They proposed creating "a city within a city," an arrangement of ten structures to include offices, a department store, a hotel, housing, and a compact plaza. Only seven were actually built, and of those, just one remains: the 11-story Cobb Building (1910), seen on the left side in this historical photo *(inset)*. Named for lumber businessman Charles H. Cobb, an investor in the Howells & Stokes project, it was originally a medical office tower but was converted into apartments in 2006. To the right in this shot is the White-Henry-Stuart Building, which was really three connected structures built between 1908 and 1915 and torn down in the late 1970s to make way for Rainier Tower, shown in the present-day photo below. Designed by University of Washington-trained architect Minoru Yamasaki (who'd previously created Manhattan's ill-fated World Trade Center), Rainier Tower rises from a shop-filled base atop what looks like a precariously thin tapered pedestal.

The Bon Marché

German-born retailer Edward Nordhoff arrived in Seattle in 1890 with his wife, Josephine. They used their life savings of $1,200 to open a dry-goods shop called the Bon Marché at First Avenue and Cedar Street in what's now Belltown. In 1896, the Nordhoffs relocated the Bon to Second Avenue and Pike Street, in the heart of the retail zone. After Edward Nordhoff died in 1899, Josephine, her new husband, and Edward's brother Rudolph set about expanding the business—and extending their downtown store to keep up. (The photo above shows the Bon Marché in 1928, after it had grown into a trio of buildings along Second Avenue between Pike and Union streets.) In 1929, the Bon moved into a new, block-size structure at Third Avenue and Pine Street, created by local architect John Graham, Sr., while its previous digs were taken over by J. C. Penney. (For many years, that Penney's outlet on Second Avenue was the chain's largest store. Penney's finally abandoned it in 1982, and the buildings were replaced in 1991 by today's Newmark Tower.) After decades of growth and chain expansion, in 1992, the Bon was sold to Cincinnati-based Federated Department Stores, Inc., owner of the Macy's and Bloomingdale's chains. In 2005, the Bon Marché stores were rebranded as Macy's.

Nordstrom

What we now recognize as the upscale department store chain known as Nordstrom began in 1901 as a shoe shop called Wallin & Nordstrom, located at Fourth Avenue and Pike Street. It was the brainchild of Swedish immigrant John W. Nordstrom, who returned from the Klondike Gold Rush after selling a disputed claim and went into business with Carl Wallin, a friend he'd met in Alaska. (In the photo below, circa 1901, Wallin, on the left, and Nordstrom stand outside the entrance to their first store.) By 1923, business was good enough that the partners opened a second shop in the University District. Five years later, John Nordstrom sold his part of the company to his sons; Wallin followed suit in 1929. By 1960, the second generation of Nordstroms owned eight shoe stores in Washington and Oregon, and their main downtown Seattle outlet—relocated to Fifth Avenue between Pike and Pine streets—was supposedly the largest shoe sales operation in the United States. In 1963, after the company purchased a Seattle women's clothing business called Best Apparel, it finally began to expand beyond footwear, adding clothes for adults and children to its line. Now managed by a fourth generation of the Nordstrom family, the company operates more than 150 stores across the nation and is known for high-quality customer service.

Frederick & Nelson

Once Seattle's most prominent department store, Frederick & Nelson was opened in 1890 by Donald E. Frederick and Nels B. Nelson. It began by peddling furniture to victims of the Great Fire of 1889 but soon expanded into ready-to-wear men's and women's fashions. By the turn of the last century, the business—then located at Second Avenue and Madison Street—offered carpeting, draperies, china, furniture, and mattresses. It even had a tea room that was staffed by 40 waitresses. In 1916, Frederick (who assumed control after Nelson died in 1907), took a chance by moving the business into a large new building (designed by John Graham, Sr.) at Fifth Avenue and Pine Street, which was then far north of the city's retail core. However, offerings such as a candy factory, a lounge for mothers with young children, and a kindergarten drew a plentiful clientele, and Frederick's dispatched mail-order goods worldwide. Donald Frederick sold out to Chicago-based Marshall Field & Company in 1929, and two decades later it opened the first major Frederick's branch outlet in what is today Bellevue Square. By 1980, Frederick & Nelson was one of America's fastest-growing retailers, but ownership changes over the next decade sent it into a death spiral. The company closed in 1992. Six years later, its Fifth Avenue flagship store was purchased and remodeled by Nordstrom as its own main outlet.

WAITING FOR "THE BIG ONE"

THE WORST EARTHQUAKE in this city's history—magnitude 7.1—struck on April 13, 1949. The deep-rooted temblor (centered between Olympia and Tacoma) lasted only about 30 seconds, yet it damaged local schools, caused power outages, and killed eight people in western Washington. In Pioneer Square, it brought ornate cornices and brick walls crashing down *(below)*. In the quake's wake, aging turrets and other downtown architectural embellishments that might someday prove hazardous were removed. (A series of walrus heads decorating the facade of the Arctic Building on Third Avenue were subsequently deprived of their original molded tusks—lest they someday skewer pedestrians—and given plastic tusks instead.) Since the '49 quake and subsequent shakers, including a 6.5-magnitude one in 1965 (which killed seven people and caused millions of dollars in damage) and a 6.8-magnitude quake in 2001 (which caused further destruction in Pioneer Square and temporarily closed the Alaskan Way Viaduct), the city has beefed up its building codes and public safety plans. Yet seismologists warn that convulsive shifts in continental plates or shallower ruptures in faults running beneath the Puget Sound area could someday cause Seattle much worse ruin.

Coliseum Theater/Banana Republic

B. Marcus Priteca was born in Scotland in 1889, came to Seattle in 1909 to visit the Alaska-Yukon-Pacific Exposition, and stayed. He's said to have designed more than 200 theaters, many of them for impresario Alexander Pantages. His Coliseum Theater at Fifth Avenue and Pike Street was opened by real-estate developer Joe Gottstein in 1916. (The top left photo shows it in February of that year, mantled by snow.) Gottstein believed the public would flock to films if only they were presented amid classy and comfortable surroundings. Priteca's answer was the 2,400-seat Italian Renaissance-flavored Coliseum, with its glazed white face, dentiled cornice, and garnishes of urns, fruit, and bullock's heads. This theater lost its half-dome entrance in 1950 and shut its doors as a movie house in 1990. Four years later, though, it was reopened as a Banana Republic store (pictured at the bottom left of this page); its exterior was refurbished but its interior (which once boasted a Turkish-style men's smoking room and an auditorium ceiling on which lights blinked out the Big Dipper's shape) was gutted and altered to accommodate merchandise.

DENNY REGRADE

During the late 19th century, Seattle pioneer Arthur Denny prospered from the sale of his extensive urban land holdings. However, he held firmly to one chunk of real estate—six acres around Second Avenue and Virginia Street, on what was then Denny Hill—believing it was an ideal spot for Washington's territorial capitol building. After Olympia beat Seattle to become the seat of Washington's government, Denny came up with another use for that property: He would build a first-class hotel there. Plans drawn by New York architect A. B. Jennings showed an opulent, five-story Victorian structure (right, circa 1906) with 240 guest rooms. Work on the inn got under way in 1889 but was halted by the nationwide Panic of 1893. Denny sold the property to real-estate broker, builder, and promoter extraordinaire James A. Moore, who completed his Washington Hotel just in time to welcome President Theodore Roosevelt in 1903. Though praised, the resort was doomed, for city engineer Reginald H. Thomson had decided to flatten Denny Hill as part of his downtown regrading project. Moore fought back, constructing a private tram to carry his guests up steep Denny Hill and proposing to erect an elegant theater on Second Avenue, right below his inn. But in 1906, he finally gave in to Thomson, who proceeded to wipe all memory of the hotel and its mount from the map. *Below:* A broad staircase wound up from the Washington Hotel's lobby to a grandiose second-floor dining room.

After the regrading of Denny Hill was completed, James A. Moore constructed two new hostelries on Second Avenue between Virginia and Stewart streets. The north end of the block is dominated by the seven-story, white-glazed-brick-fronted Moore Theatre & Hotel *(right)*. Opened in 1907 and designed by Edwin W. Houghton, it features a performance venue that was hailed by the *Seattle Post-Intelligencer* as "the finest playhouse in the great domain West of the Mississippi River." (The Moore is currently the oldest theater in Seattle still fulfilling its original role.) At the opposite end of the block, and climbing 14 stories, is The Josephinum (formerly the New Washington Hotel), which was designed by St. Louis architects William Eames and Thomas Young and is now a Catholic home for the low-income elderly.

Before Reginald Thomson began tearing away at Denny Hill, it rose steeply to the north of Pine Street between Second and Fifth avenues (with its high point near Moore's Washington Hotel) and then descended northward toward Cedar Street. West of Second, the land dropped abruptly down to Elliott Bay. Regrading took place in three stages, beginning in 1898. Using jets of water pumped from Lake Union and, later, power shovels, Thomson's crews pushed dirt and rock onto the Elliott Bay tidelands, building up the waterfront while creating level, buildable land in Belltown. Residents who balked at relinquishing their homes in the regrade zone were isolated high atop "spite mounds" (above, circa 1910) as engineers dug around their property. Those otherworldly monoliths didn't disappear entirely until 1911. Twenty more years would pass before the Denny Regrade was completed.

THE IMPROBABLE DREAM

WITH THE REGRADING of steep slopes on the north end of downtown came plans for developing that new commercial acreage. The most ambitious of these was presented by civil engineer Virgil G. Bogue. Hired in 1910 to create a comprehensive strategy for Seattle's growth and heavily influenced by the "City Beautiful Movement," Bogue proposed building a new, architecturally unified civic center in the Denny Regrade area. It would have included a courthouse, a federal building, an art museum, a library, and a city hall topped with a 15-story tower. These would all face a European-style plaza at Fourth Avenue and Blanchard Street and be connected (via a broad tree-shaded boulevard) to a railroad station at the southwest corner of Lake Union. Beyond that, Bogue's plan featured an intricate rapid-transit system, with 33 miles of electric-powered subways and 27 miles of elevated trains; a five-mile-long commuter transit tunnel beneath Lake Washington; and new parks everywhere, with all of Mercer Island set aside as "a people's playground."

When first unveiled in September 1911, Bogue's ideas (as pictured in the plans below) were heartily endorsed. But they quickly lost support as naysayers complained of the plan's cost, and wealthy businessmen rallied against a project that would have shifted government offices out of downtown's south end, where those capitalists had so many real-estate investments. In 1912, negative press finally convinced Seattle voters to reject Bogue's plan by an almost two-to-one margin.

BELLTOWN

Once rather squalid and rundown, the district known as Belltown has become considerably more chic over the last two decades. It takes its name from William Bell, who with his wife, Sarah, arrived at Alki Point with the Denny party in 1851. In the spring of 1852, William and Sarah staked out adjoining donation land claims of 160 acres apiece at the north end of what would become downtown Seattle. But after the Native American uprisings of 1856, they fled to California. William Bell returned alone in the early 1870s, following his wife's demise. By that time, his lands had appreciated significantly, and he set about making improvements, including erecting the Bell Hotel, a four-story, mansard-roofed landmark at Front (now First Avenue) and Bell streets. That hotel was completed in 1883.

In 1887, William Bell died after several years of mental deterioration. He was buried by his son, Austin, who thereafter sought to continue his father's work. Austin also began planning construction of a brick apartment building next door to his father's hotel, to be designed by the not-yet-renowned Elmer H. Fisher. However, Austin was desperately afraid that he'd succumb to the same psychological decay that had afflicted his father, so he shot himself to death in April 1889. Though devastated, his wife, Eva, decided to finish the Victorian Gothic edifice that Fisher had designed on her husband's behalf. William Bell's hotel (shown at right, circa 1898) was demolished in the 1930s. The Austin A. Bell Building was abandoned for many years after 1939 and was damaged by fire in 1981. But in 1997, its distinctive facade was preserved as the front of a modern condominium structure.

During the 1930s and '40s, the Trianon Ballroom at Third Avenue and Wall Street was the largest dance hall in the Pacific Northwest. Designed by architect Warren Milner and meant to resemble a Spanish castle, this segregated club was opened in 1926 by cabaret entrepreneur John Savage. The Trianon hosted most of the era's big-name swing bandleaders, both black and white, from Benny Goodman and Duke Ellington to Count Basie, Les Brown, Harry James, and Tommy and Jimmy Dorsey.

Admission to the Trianon (shown at left, circa 1935) cost twenty-five cents. The springy maple dance floor could accommodate 5,000 people; there were 16 balconies for privacy-craving lovers; and a giant silver clamshell sheltered the bandstand. During World War II, it wasn't unusual to see 2,000 well-dressed Seattleites standing outside at 1 A.M., waiting to enter. However, the Trianon closed in 1956. It was renovated as office space in the 1980s.

The Crystal Pool building (above, circa 1927) at Second Avenue and Lenora Street was a first-class recreational facility opened in 1915 by local lumber mill owner C. D. Stimson. Designed in Italian Renaissance style by theater architect B. Marcus Priteca, it boasted an ornate terra-cotta facade, playfully decorated with dolphins and tridents. The salt water that filled the glass-roofed pool was piped up from Elliott Bay and then heated and chlorinated. Seating for 1,500 people surrounded the basin. Although initially popular, the pool was closed in the 1930s. The building later hosted boxing matches, and in 1943 became a Pentecostal church, with a floor laid over the pool. Its domed marquee was removed in the 1950s. All that remains of Priteca's natatorium today is the arched arcade, which has been incorporated into a 23-story condominium tower called the Cristalla *(left)*, opened in 2005.

ABOVE IT ALL

Nobody could accuse the adjoining neighborhoods of Queen Anne and Lower Queen Anne, located just north of downtown, of failing to reach for the sky. Indeed, over the last century and a half they've demonstrated nothing so clearly as their lofty ambitions. Queen Anne Hill, the city's second-highest peak (after West Seattle's appropriately named High Point), became an early home to the mighty and the moneyed—the people most comfortable looking down on the rest of the city. But even they were impressed when, in the 1960s, organizers of Seattle's second world's fair erected the Space Needle, which was about 150 feet taller than the hill next door.

Planning for the fair began in the mid-1950s, and some civic leaders proposed hosting it as early as 1959, a convenient half century after the city's first such international spectacle, which was held on the University of Washington campus (see Chapter 6). The site they ultimately chose, on the south side of Queen Anne Hill, had been known by 19th-century settlers as "Potlatch Meadow," under the (apparently mistaken) belief that it had once hosted Native American tribal ceremonies. Later, it was the province of dairy cattle and sweetbriar rose bushes. Not until the second quarter of the 20th century did that acreage begin to acquire urban attributes. In 1928, the Civic Auditorium was built there (it would later become an opera house and was more recently replaced by Seattle Opera's grand McCaw Hall). The U.S. Army constructed an armory nearby in 1939

(it's now the Center House at Seattle Center), and nine years after that, the Seattle School District raised Memorial Stadium as a venue for high-school football games. The site was considered ideal for a world's fair, as planners knew the fair would leave behind at least several permanent structures to supplement those already in place.

FAIR PLAY

What came to be called the Century 21 Exposition (suggestive of its forward-looking concept) didn't open until the spring of 1962, but the delay of a few years hardly dampened public enthusiasm. People from all over the world came to Seattle to attend the fair. They arrived hoping to visit the "Spacearium," sponsored by Boeing, which simulated an express tour of Earth's solar system. Other enticements included a ride on the

Above: The World's Fair made the cover of *Life.*

Left: The Space Needle soars over the monorail in this aerial view of the 1962 World's Fair.

see-through "Bubbleator" or the ultra-modern Alweg Monorail (perhaps in the company of singer Elvis Presley, who was in town to shoot a film titled *It Happened at the World's Fair*). And, of course, all attendees were anxious to gaze up at the 602-foot-tall Space Needle, a skyline icon that is this city's equivalent to San Francisco's Golden Gate Bridge or London's Big Ben. "Back when we were in school, if you wanted attention, you put up your hand. That is what the Space Needle will do for the fair and Seattle," boasted Joe Gandy, a local Ford salesman and civic booster who, as president of the Century 21 Expo, not only got Seattle—and its notable Needle—on the cover of *Life* magazine, but also brought the city the sort of recognition it had not enjoyed since the stampede for Klondike riches.

The former fairgrounds are now Seattle Center, a 74-acre aggregate of theaters, public exhibition spaces, and sports arenas. The Center is the site of annual festivals, including a fall arts and music extravaganza called Bumbershoot, and a smaller, funkier Memorial Day weekend celebration known as the Northwest Folklife Festival. It's also become a popular destination for Sunday strollers and protestors in search of media coverage. If Pioneer Square can be called Seattle's front room and Pike Place Market its kitchen, then Seattle Center is certainly the city's comfortable backyard.

SPLENDID RETREATS

Queen Anne Hill sits above the fray. Residents may relish their views of Elliott Bay and Lake Union, and of Lower Queen Anne's ethnic restaurants, office termitaries, and the famous rotating Elephant Car Wash sign—a *pink* elephant sign, no less. But they have their own backyards, thank you, and a good number of those sit behind elegant homes once owned by people after whom city streets are now named. Although many of its capitalist castles have been toppled or subdivided over the decades, Queen Anne remains isolated by choice, its more than 30,000 residents pleased that their neighborhood (unlike another retreat for deep-pocketed Seattleites of old, Capitol Hill) is still family-oriented, picturesque, and fairly laid-back even in the early 21st century.

Still more secluded is Magnolia, a sparsely populated (with fewer than 19,200 inhabitants), yet physically immense, community located on a peninsula northwest of Queen Anne. As the story goes, this neighborhood takes its name from an error made by Captain George Vancouver, who while sailing past it in the 18th century, misidentified the madrona trees rimming the peninsula's southern bluffs. Connected by only three bridges to the rest of the city, Magnolia maintains a small-town feel. As its residents like to say, people don't pass through Magnolia to get anywhere; they come for a purpose, whether they live in one of the district's mostly single-family homes or are visiting Discovery Park, a mammoth and environmentally varied tract once dominated by a U.S. Army base.

On the other hand, Lake Union buzzes with activity. High-end restaurants, houseboat communities, annual sailboat races, a maritime history center—all vie for notice around the once-industrialized basin east of Queen Anne Hill. And the future promises even more bustle, as the lake's south end thickens with new condominium developments, office complexes, and headquarters for life-science organizations where researchers tackle their own lofty ambitions.

Above: Lower Queen Anne's landmark Elephant Car Wash sign

Right: View of the Seattle skyline over Lake Union

CENTURY 21 EXPO/ SEATTLE CENTER

If the Alaska-Yukon-Pacific Exposition (A-Y-P) of 1909 proved that Seattle had shed its frontier wooliness, then the Century 21 Exposition of 1962 showed just how anxious this city was to be counted among the world's foremost metropolises. Significant arm-twisting was necessary to convince the Bureau of International Expositions (BIE) in Paris that Seattle deserved a second world's fair. State and federal officials were equally reticent to fund the enterprise. But by April 21, 1962, when President John F. Kennedy pressed a golden telegraph key to start the festivities (the same key with which President William Howard Taft had signaled the opening of the A-Y-P 53 years earlier), it was obvious that Seattle knew how to throw a planetwide party. In fact, the Century 21 blowout was one of the last world's fairs to make a profit, drawing close to ten million visitors.

That six-month-long extravaganza was a late blooming of innocence and optimism in a century troubled by Cold War. Exhibits were preoccupied with a fantasy of what the future might hold, complete with simulated rides into outer space and concept houses full of disposable everything. Architecturally, the fair *(right)* was like *The Jetsons* come to life, with its sleek silver monorail, its lofty Space Needle, and a six-acre U.S. Science Pavilion.

Architect Minoru Yamasaki, together with the local firm Naramore, Bain, Brady & Johanson (later NBBJ), designed the Science Pavilion. Originally comprising half a dozen interconnected white buildings centered on a pool-filled courtyard, the Pavilion (top, circa 1962) featured 100 exhibits focused on the history and potential of scientific endeavors, spread out over three football fields worth of floor space. That pavilion is now the eight-building Pacific Science Center, home to hundreds of permanent, hands-on displays and host to traveling exhibits on everything from Chinese history and the Dead Sea Scrolls to the 1912 sinking of the *Titanic*. A planetarium and two IMAX theaters keep the crowds coming.

Seattle Monorail

Proposals to create an elevated mass-transit line through Seattle date to the early 20th century, but it took the 1962 World's Fair to bring such lofty plans down to Earth. Hoping to capitalize on the exposition's space-age theme and create additional "photo opportunities" for the press, Century 21 organizers signed with the Swedish company Alweg Rapid Transit Systems (which had developed Disneyland's monorail) to construct a 1.2-mile-long monorail system from the fairgrounds to the downtown shopping district. That line *(right)* opened in March 1962. After the expo closed, the city took over the system and has been running it ever since, carrying some 400,000 passengers annually on two trains between what are now Seattle Center and Westlake Center at Fifth Avenue and Pine Street.

Japanese Village

A variety of foreign nations mounted exhibits at this fair, including Great Britain, Mexico, Canada, Peru, Sweden, India, Denmark, the Republic of China, and Japan. But the Pacific Northwest's historic and commercial ties to Asia were also recognized in the development of a Japanese Village *(above)*, located on what was known as "Show Street" in the fairgrounds' northeast corner. Show Street offered a Parisian wax museum, Sid and Marty Krofft's adults-only puppet show, and Gracie Hansen's leggy, topless Las Vegas–style floor show. Visitors stopped by the Japanese Village to see formal tea ceremonies, watch pearl divers retrieve real gem-bearing mollusks, and sample "exotic" meals of rice and fish. *Inset:* Every fair must have its fairest of them all, and in the case of the Seattle expo, that beauty was Pat Dzejachok, a Bellevue model who in August 1962 was proclaimed Miss Century 21.

The Bubbleator

Contributing to the fair's futuristic theme, the Washington State Coliseum (today's Key Arena sports stadium) housed a $1.6-million "World of Tomorrow" show. Visitors rode a 150-passenger plexiglas elevator, called the "Bubbleator," up into a honeycomb of aluminum cubes where synchronized recordings and film and slide montages forecast the lifestyles of the 21st century. Among the predictions: disposable dishes, plastic clothes, foods made from cotton and wood wastes, machines to transmit correspondence, videophones, private heliports, 24-hour work weeks, and astronomical salaries of $12,000 a year. Following the exposition's run, the Bubbleator was relocated to another building on the fair site, but was eventually sold to an employee of the *Seattle Post-Intelligencer,* who converted it into a greenhouse at his Des Moines home. *Inset:* A 1973 flyer appeals to Seattleites to prevent the Bubbleator's removal from the Seattle Center.

L-C   4390   mf
Library in the Coliseum

The UNIVAC Computer

Information at your fingertips! Well, sort of. The American Library Association offered its own vision of the future with an eight-ton UNIVAC computer that it said would revolutionize data collection. Visitors to the Coliseum were invited to ask well-dressed librarians questions, the answers to which would be generated by this technological behemoth (preprogrammed with "quotations from great books, gazetteer information, and bibliographical material"). Among the folks who were first exposed to computers at this expo was an unusually gifted six-year-old Seattleite named Bill Gates—the future chairman of Microsoft—who would remember the Century 21 Fair as "a huge event, a neat deal."

Experience Music Project

In the decades since the 1962 World's Fair closed down, that Lower Queen Anne site—now Seattle Center—has changed considerably, with new buildings, sculptures, and other attractions being peppered in among the originals. One of the most controversial additions was the Experience Music Project (EMP), financed by Microsoft co-founder Paul Allen. It grew out of billionaire Allen's longstanding fondness for the music of Seattle-born rock guitarist/singer Jimi Hendrix, whom he'd first seen perform during a 1968 concert at what's now the Mercer Arena at Seattle Center. Over time, Allen amassed an impressive collection of rock-'n'-roll memorabilia, which he hoped to house at the new EMP. To design the museum, he hired Los Angeles architect Frank O. Gehry, recognized for his warped structural forms. Gehry came up with a billowing, polychromatic structure covered in stainless steel and aluminum shingles. In 2004, the EMP incorporated the Science Fiction Museum and Hall of Fame, which features such artifacts as Captain James T. Kirk's command chair from *Star Trek* and a model of the Death Star from *Star Wars*. The monorail passes directly through the EMP.

The Gayway

Immediately south of the fair's Show Street was the more child-friendly "Gayway," stocked with some 20 amusement rides, many of them space-oriented. Youngsters unimpressed by earnest scientific exhibits elsewhere in the park found their thrills on the Trip to Mars, the Meteor, and the gondola-style Sky Ride. Or they emptied their pockets of change to ride the Geister Express, a two-level ride through a spooky Swiss nightmare scene, and have their breaths taken away as they rounded the tight corners of the Wild Mouse roller coaster. In the photo above, the two boys in the front are wearing examples of the colorful, brimmed felt hats that were sold as souvenirs of this fair (usually monogrammed with the owner's name).

QUEEN ANNE

At 456 feet high, Queen Anne Hill, located north of Seattle Center, is the loftiest of this city's seven or eight prominent mounts. Claims to property on its slopes were staked shortly after white settlers first arrived in this area, but it wasn't until the 1880s that the prominence saw significant residential development. After being referred to for years as Galer Hill or Eden Hill, it was finally christened "Queen Anne" in 1885 in recognition of the architectural style prevalent in many homes lining its then dirt streets. Boosting the neighborhood's growth was a cable (later electric) railway that ran north along First Avenue from Pioneer Square and scaled the 20-percent incline of Temperance Street, today's Queen Anne Avenue. That climb was made possible by the 1890s installation of two 16-ton counterbalance cars in a narrow tunnel beneath the tracks. Streetcars needing to ascend Queen Anne Avenue hooked onto a cable connected to the counterbalance at the hill's summit and were pulled upward (at eight miles an hour) as that counterbalance descended. Similarly, cars heading downhill used their weight to pull the underground counterbalance back up to the hill's crest. This system was discontinued in 1940, when electric and diesel buses replaced the streetcars, but locals still call Queen Anne Avenue on the south side of this hill "the Counterbalance."

With timber a plentiful commodity in 19th-century Seattle, it's not surprising that some people chose to build log cabins rather than conventional homes of milled lumber. However, most of those cabins didn't look like this top-heavy specimen, constructed in 1889 (and shown at left, circa 1953) at the intersection of Queen Anne Avenue and Republican Street. It served as a real-estate office for Edward Lindsley and David Denny. The former moved west from Wisconsin around 1875 and married Abbie Denny in Seattle. She was the daughter of David Denny, who in 1851 was one of the original homesteaders at West Seattle. In 1853, Denny and his wife, the former Louisa Boren, claimed 640 acres of land stretching from today's Seattle Center east to Lake Union and as far south as present Denny Way.

Kinnear Park

In the late 1880s, as Seattleites began to recognize the value of local park development, some of George C. Kinnear's neighbors urged him to sell the city a 14-acre wedge of forested land on the southwest slope of Queen Anne Hill, offering panoramic vistas of Puget Sound and the Olympic Mountains. He soon did so—for $1. By the early '90s, that park was already taking shape, with contoured walkways, a lily pond, prolific plantings of flowers and shrubs, and footbridges. Visitors to that park in the early 20th century also found a "rustic parachute trellis seat" (pictured in the postcard above) made of cedar bark, which from afar looked like a freakishly oversize mushroom. Today, Kinnear Park (shown at present day below) remains a peaceful escape from the city's bustle, though its scenic outlook is now marred by a Port of Seattle grain elevator on the waterfront.

Kinnear Mansion

Midwesterner George C. Kinnear purchased land on the south side of Queen Anne Hill during a visit to this city in 1874, using money his mother had put aside from the paychecks he received as a Civil War soldier. Four years later, he moved his family to Seattle and went into the real-estate business. Kinnear also served as the treasurer of a local power company and promoted construction of the first wagon road through Snoqualmie Pass in the Cascade Mountains. In 1885, Kinnear built this Queen Anne–style dwelling (above, circa 1900) designed by Syracuse, New York, architects James H. Kirby and James A. Randall, near what's now the corner of Queen Anne Avenue and Aloha Street. Although it was light on Victorian-era gingerbreading, the Kinnear mansion featured an abundance of gables and balconies, and the grounds included decorative fountains fed by a spring behind the house. The mansion's turret was a landmark until the residence was taken down in 1958 to make way for a retirement home.

Highland Drive

During the early 20th century, an address on Highland Drive—about halfway up the west side of Queen Anne Hill—was a mark of prestige. Mansions were positively commonplace there, housing the families of lumber barons, bankers, and at least one bombastic newspaper publisher. The last was Alden J. Blethen, who had previously been a lawyer in Maine. Blethen reached Seattle right before the Klondike Gold Rush and created what's now *The Seattle Times*. Blethen was so pleased with his pillared manse and the neighborhood surrounding it that for many years he paid out of his own pocket to have Highland Drive gaslit at night. Not far away was the home of Martin D. Ballard (shown at left shortly after construction and pictured below in the present day), who organized the Seattle Hardware Company and had a hand in founding the National Bank of Commerce. Ballard commissioned architect Emil DeNeuf to create this Colonial/Georgian Revival–style residence in 1901. About a decade later, it was bought by lawyer James B. Howe and still later was converted into apartments. The Ballard-Howe home has been listed as a Seattle Landmark since 1979.

Alexander Hall, Seattle Pacific University

Seattle Seminary was founded by the Free Methodist Church in 1891, and within two years it had fully occupied this four-story red brick building (shown below, circa 1915) on the north side of Queen Anne Hill. The fortresslike structure was designed by John Parkinson, an English-born architect who arrived in Seattle in January 1889—just months ahead of the city's Great Fire, which would provide him with significant commissions to rebuild downtown. (He may be best remembered for creating the Interurban Building at Yesler Way and Occidental Avenue South in Pioneer Square.) Parkinson later relocated to Southern California, where he gained renown with his work on the Los Angeles City Hall, the Los Angeles Memorial Coliseum, and that city's prized 1939 Union Station. Meanwhile, Seattle Seminary became Seattle Pacific College in 1915 and Seattle Pacific University in 1977. It now occupies more than 40 acres, featuring some of the oldest trees in the city. Parkinson's original seminary still stands but is now known as Alexander Hall, in honor of the school's first principal (and later president), Alexander Beers.

Queen Anne High School

Opened in 1909, the Beaux Arts–style Queen Anne High School (shown above shortly after opening and pictured at left in the present day) was the work of James Stephen. A cabinetmaker turned designer, Stephen served from 1899 to 1908 as the Seattle School District's resident architect. Queen Anne High School, on Second Avenue North between Galer and Lee streets, was among his most massive works and remains the most visible landmark atop Queen Anne Hill. It was enlarged twice—in 1929 and 1955—to accommodate climbing enrollments; the modifications were less grandiose and classically oriented than the original school building. The school district closed the doors of Queen Anne High in 1981, but six years later—after a pricey, historically respected conversion—it was reopened as an apartment building. It's now on the National Register of Historic Places.

MAGNOLIA

In terms of acreage, Magnolia, at the north end of Elliott Bay, is the city's second largest neighborhood after West Seattle. However, it's largely residential, with a small business district (known as "The Village") along West McGraw Street between 32nd and 35th avenues. Its other principal attractions are giant Discovery Park and Fishermen's Terminal. The latter of those is located at the south end of the Ballard Bridge on Salmon Bay. It was established by the Port of Seattle in 1913 as a new home base for commercial fishers whose traditional moorages were jeopardized by construction of the Lake Washington Ship Canal. (The photo below, taken around 1918, shows some of those fishers checking and mending gill nets.) Expanded in 1946 and rebuilt during the late 1980s, Fishermen's Terminal now serves some 600 commercial fishing vessels, as well as pleasure craft, which have been allowed to dock at this terminal since 2001. In addition to being an important commercial venture (Washington is the second largest seafood producer in the United States outside of Alaska), the moorage provides ample entertainment, as boats from the North Pacific fleet dock here to unload and sell parts of their catches to sightseeing consumers. Also prominent here is the Seattle Fishermen's Memorial, a tall bronze and gold sculpture by Seattleite Ron Petty that was dedicated in 1988 and honors the memory of 500 local fishers who were lost at sea during the last century.

Above: Even consumers who've never held a fishing rod enjoy Fishermen's Terminal for its restaurants and fresh seafood market.

Fort Lawton

With the late 19th century bringing significant growth to the Puget Sound area, U.S. military planners pushed for new fortifications capable of protecting local cities from hostile incursions. Eleven sites were identified, including—at the north end of the Sound—what became Fort Worden and Fort Flagler near Port Townsend on the Olympic Peninsula and Fort Casey on Whidbey Island, just east across Admiralty Inlet. Those were considered the first and second lines of defense and were armed with huge guns. Magnolia Bluff was designated as a third line of protection. Eventually, 703 acres of public and private land were relinquished to the War Department for the new Fort Lawton, and soldiers began arriving there in 1899. However, local expectations of a major garrison being raised were dashed, and guns were installed only temporarily. Some 20,000 troops were stationed at Fort Lawton during World War II, and German and Italian prisoners of war were incarcerated there. In 1968, the Department of Defense considered installing antiballistic missiles at Fort Lawton, but the plan was nixed through the intervention of Washington's junior U.S. senator, Democrat Henry M. Jackson. Three years later, the army turned over 534 acres of Fort Lawton to the city of Seattle for development as a park, maintaining only a small army reserve headquarters, which is expected to close before this decade is out.

Discovery Park

The 534-acre tract of old Fort Lawton that Seattle received from the American military was dedicated in 1973 as Discovery Park, named after the ship British explorer Captain George Vancouver sailed into Puget Sound in 1792. The largest of Seattle's public parks, Discovery Park is veined by more than seven miles of hiking trails, including a 2.8-mile loop route that's especially popular with runners. There's also an art-filled Native American cultural center on the property, built in 1977, and a small lighthouse opened in 1881. However, most of Discovery Park has been left wild. It's said to harbor more than 160 species of birds and is rich in stands of red cedar and big-leaf maple trees. Harbor seals and California sea lions can be seen along the easily accessible shoreline.

LAKE UNION

It's said that midwesterner David Denny, who reached Puget Sound in 1851 ahead of his elder brother Arthur's pioneering Denny Party, was the first white man to claim land on Lake Union, the 580-acre freshwater basin just north of downtown. However, it fell to another early settler, Thomas Mercer, to name that lake. Mercer was Seattle's first teamster, hauling timber from the surrounding hills down to Yesler's Mill. He was also the older brother of Asa Mercer, who would later engineer the importation of marriageable maidens for lonely Seattle bachelors. Until 1854, Lake Union was known by its Chinook jargon label, *tenas chuck* ("little water"), while today's Lake Washington, to the east, was called *hyas chuck* ("big water"). But during a Fourth of July picnic that year, held at Thomas Mercer's farm south of the lake, Mercer proposed that *hyas chuck* be renamed in honor of the general-president who had made their holiday possible—George Washington—and that the smaller body of water be christened Lake Union. This designation reflected Mercer's belief that Lake Union would one day be part of a canal linking Lake Washington with Puget Sound—a canal that would finally become a reality 63 years later. *Right:* Looking west from Capitol Hill, across Lake Union toward Queen Anne Hill, circa 1895.

Brace and Hergert Mill

Engineer Virgil G. Bogue, who in 1911 proposed that a new civic center be constructed in the Denny Regrade area, also suggested raising a grand Central Station at the south end of Lake Union to serve railroads, ferries, and a rapid-transit system. Like so many others, he thought the lakeshore was best suited to industrial development. Its south end was already dominated by the Brace and Hergert Mill (formerly the Western Mill), which opened in 1882 and was purchased two years later by David Denny. At that time, Denny was one of the city's richest men. His sawmill, located near the corner of present-day Mercer Street and Westlake Avenue, was part of a business empire that included real-estate holdings and, eventually, a streetcar line from downtown to the University District. But the Panic of 1893 forced Denny into bankruptcy, and in 1899 the mill was purchased by two former employees, John S. Brace and Frank Hergert. Destroyed by fire in 1909, it was rebuilt on a landfill just north of its original position. The mill (shown at left, circa 1910) was sold to the Stimson Timber Company in 1921, and in 1940 it was replaced by the U.S. Naval Reserve Building on Terry Avenue, now a special events venue.

Gas Works Park

The 20-acre promontory at the north end of Lake Union where Gas Works Park now spreads was once a popular, wooded picnic spot for Victorian-era Seattleites. In the early 20th century, the famous Olmsted Brothers landscaping firm of Massachusetts—which had been hired by local city fathers to develop a comprehensive plan for Seattle parks development—suggested that the outcropping "be secured as a local park, because of its advantages for commanding views over the lake and for boating, and for a playground." But before any such plans could be instituted, the Seattle Gas Light Company (later simply the Seattle Gas Company) began purchasing the property. By 1907, it had opened a plant capable of generating gas from coal, which could then be used in residential cooking, heating, and refrigeration. That plant showered soot over the adjacent Wallingford neighborhood until the 1930s, when it switched its process from coal to petroleum. By the time Seattle Gas (shown at left, circa 1951) ceased belching pollution in 1956, it had caked the promontory with hydrocarbon contaminants. Six years later, the city agreed to buy the abandoned gas works for more than $1.3 million, hoping to turn it into the park the Olmsteds had imagined.

In 1970, Richard Haag, a professor with the University of Washington's Architecture and Planning Department, was hired to create a master plan for redeveloping the gas works site. His proposal called for extensive landscaping but also for retaining a few towers and pipes from the old industrial plant as historic, if admittedly bizarre, relics. At the same time, decades of industrial poisons had to be leached from the soil. Gas Works Park was opened in 1974. Today, children play all over what remains of the rusted factory (right), visit a giant sundial (created by artists Charles Greening and Kim Lazare in 1979) embedded at the summit of a manufactured Great Mound nearby, and fly kites on the extensive park lawns.

The Beginning of Boeing

William E. Boeing, the Detroit-born son of a wealthy German mining engineer, left Yale University in 1903 and came to the Pacific Northwest to get into the timber industry. By 1908 he'd made a fortune and settled in Seattle, where he discovered flying. On July 4, 1914, he and his best friend, Navy officer G. Conrad Westervelt, went to Lake Washington, where they met a barnstorming pilot who was selling people chances behind the wheel of his pontoon plane. Boeing paid his money, strapped on a pair of goggles, and lifted off with the pilot beside him. It was the first of several flights he and Westervelt took that day. Shortly thereafter, Boeing went to Los Angeles to take flying lessons, and upon his return the two friends started building an airplane of their own in a hangar-boathouse on the east side of Lake Union. In June 1916, Boeing piloted their new two-winged, single-engine float plane, called the B&W *Bluebill*, above the lake. The next month, he and Westervelt incorporated the Pacific Aero-Products Company, which—following a move from Lake Union to the Duwamish River south of Seattle—became the Boeing Airplane Company. *Right:* An early Boeing seaplane lifts off from in front of the Seattle Gas Company.

Ford Motor Company Assembly Plant

In 1913, this five-story brick-and-glass building *(left)* was opened as a Ford Motor Company assembly plant on the corner of Fairview Avenue North and Valley Street, in south Lake Union. Designed by architect John Graham, Sr., it was one of several facilities located across the country where Model T cars—which remained in production from 1908 through 1927—were put together. In addition to this plant, Ford built a boardinghouse for its employees on Queen Anne Avenue between Roy and Mercer streets, which is now the boutique MarQueen Hotel. Car-assembly operations were shifted away from this structure in the early 1930s. Since 1998, it's been a city of Seattle landmark and today houses a public storage facility.

Left: This houseboat dates to 1905.

Floating Homes

Shacks built on floats began appearing along the Elliott Bay waterfront toward the close of the 19th century, mainly housing loggers from the camps around Seattle. It took another half-dozen years for houseboats to flourish on industrial Lake Union; yet by 1914, there were several hundred of them. Lake Union floating homes grew in number during the 1920s, built by people who made their living from the water—fishers, boatmakers, and a few bootleggers. Floating homes multiplied still further—to more than 2,000—during the Great Depression, to help fill a need for cheap housing. After World War II, a bohemian crowd moved into Seattle's remaining houseboat colonies, inciting public calls for their destruction before they turned into slums. But campaigns by floating-home owners to solve sewage-disposal problems, improve "classic" houseboats and construct sturdy newer ones, and secure their rights to remain on the lakefront have led to a reappraisal. There are now some 500 legal floating homes on Lake Union and Portage Bay, some of them as expensive as anything you'll find on land. For instance, when the houseboat used in the 1993 film *Sleepless in Seattle* went on the market in 2008, its asking price was $2.5 million.

THE UMBRELLA MAN

NO, THIS IS NOT the mascot of Bumbershoot, Seattle's annual Labor Day arts and entertainment festival. It's Robert W. Patten, a familiar if eccentric figure on the city's streets during the early 20th century. He claimed to have been born in 1811 but actually took his first breath in 1832 and arrived here around 1900, sporting an umbrella-shape hat and mosquito netting that he said had protected him during his gold-prospecting days in Mexico's Yucatan. Patten claimed a lot of things, really: that he was a Civil War veteran, that he'd hunted with Kit Carson, had been adopted by the Upper Midwest's Winnebago Indians, and saved explorer John C. Frémont from certain death in the Rockies. It was hard to know what was true, other than that he lived in a houseboat on Lake Union and inspired a *Seattle Times* cartoon feature, beginning in 1909, that bestowed wit and weather forecasts on its readers. After years spent fishing and fixing things (often umbrellas), Patten died in 1913.

HEAD FOR THE HILLS

In the beginning, the hills west of Elliott Bay were greater than early Seattleites' determination to conquer them. But that wasn't true for long. One of the first evolutionary steps toward expanding this town beyond its waterfront-hugging origins was to clear the surrounding heights of towering timber—a task undertaken with great relish (and the prospect of great reward) by mill owner Henry Yesler and others. Buildable acreage wouldn't attract many buyers, though, unless adequate transportation to those new districts was provided. Some initial attempts to connect Seattle's nascent eastern suburbs with downtown were crude but nonetheless proved significant.

This old black-and-white photograph, dated 1887 *(left)*, shows a horse-drawn stagecoach that worked the rough network of trails linking the small inner city with what we now know as the Capitol Hill neighborhood. "The line ended back in the woods where Harvard Ave. is today," reads a note scrawled on the back of the image. Riding such a wooden conveyance must have been quite an adventure and would have taken hours rather than the short time necessary to cover the same route over today's smooth-surfaced roads. No wonder the hills east of downtown were so sparsely settled until the 1890s, when technology and the increasingly busy, noisy, and malodorous business district convinced many people that they would be better off living farther from the center of things.

RIDING THE RAILS

More important and longer lasting were the cable railway lines that began snaking out from Pioneer Square in the 1880s and '90s. One of those ran northeast along then-narrow Madison Street, carrying passengers to a distant residential subdivision and a budding public park on the western shore of Lake Washington, where musical concerts and some of Seattle's earliest professional baseball games could be enjoyed. It wasn't as scenic, though, as the line stretching east to today's Leschi neighborhood, south of Madison Park. Although much of the land through which those iron rails passed had been logged off, there were still deep ravines to contend with. The railway's owners didn't wish to run their small, open-sided grip cars up and down steep slopes—thus increasing the time

First Hill Residence District, Seattle, Wash.

Above: As this postcard from the 20th century shows, Seattle's near-east neighborhoods strove for elegance and exclusivity.

it took to travel the length of the route; instead, they constructed soaring trestles over the gorges. One, known as the Jackson Street trestle, was an engineering marvel, tall and beautiful—the sort of woven wooden overpass that has become famous in Old West movies and once symbolized humankind's triumph over nature. But because the railway company sought to save a buck or two, the trestle stood no chance of outlasting its builders. A near disaster occurred in the summer of 1890, when a particularly forceful gust of wind struck a cable car at the top of the trestle's grade, rocking the car so dangerously that passengers actually leapt from the moving vehicle onto the railing that bordered the viaduct on both sides. Apparently, the gripman (conductor) managed to remain at his post, "careening wildly down to the lake front," where wooden ties tossed desperately across the tracks finally put an end to the car's mad rush. That trestle was abandoned in the early 1890s, and the cable car's route changed.

A CAPITOL IDEA

Getting people to and from the communities and resorts that sprouted east of downtown was one thing; convincing them to invest in land there was another. Among those who enjoyed the most success in that latter task was James A. Moore, a Nova Scotia-born real-estate

tycoon who moved to Seattle from Denver, Colorado, just before the Great Fire of 1889. Moore proceeded to buy and then divide huge tracts of land for sale. His foremost acquisition may have been a 160-acre parcel adjoining Volunteer Park, which would become one of the city's best-landscaped public retreats. The developer paid $225,000 for that tract—which the *Seattle Argus* called the last of the "high-grade resident properties to be platted." Moore endeavored to ensure that his new development had the

Above: Postcard of the Lake Washington Boulevard Bridge at Leschi Park

finest pedigree by prohibiting construction there of any home worth less than $3,000—a large sum at the time. That he expected great things of this neighborhood, which had long been called Broadway Hill, is emphasized by the fact that he gave it the more exalted moniker "Capitol Hill"—either after an exclusive

section of Denver or because he hoped that the state capitol might be relocated from Olympia to a five-acre section of his property.

AGING GRACEFULLY

No longer considered distant suburbs, east-of-downtown neighborhoods have become integral to Seattle's urban life over the last century. First Hill and Capitol Hill appeal with their plenitude of restaurants, stylish shops, and preserved architectural landmarks. (The Harvard-Belmont Historic District on the west slope of Capitol Hill is the only historic landmark residential area in the city.) The Central District was once dominated by African Americans, who were so agreeably accommodated in Seattle during the late 19th century that this city's most prominent black-owned newspaper encouraged "the colored people of this country" to move here en masse. But after a period of decline in the late 1900s, the "CD" is now a rapidly gentrifying quarter, its old homes sheltering an increasing number of young families. In the meantime, the park-suffused communities along Lake Washington Boulevard have aged gracefully. Today, they provide pleasant summer drives and picnic stops in addition to a few famous sites—among them, grunge musician-songwriter Kurt Cobain's former home near Viretta Park, in the Denny-Blaine district.

Right: Jackson Street cable car trestle, circa 1889

FIRST HILL

If ever a prominent mount possessed a prosaic moniker, it is Seattle's First Hill, east of Pioneer Square. This was the first hill city founders contended with after relocating to the east side of Elliott Bay. Most saw the prominence as an impediment to their village's growth and feared the "throngs of Indians" said to be concealed there. (It was from First Hill that the 1856 "Battle of Seattle" was launched.) However, sawmill owner Henry Yesler read dollars signs in the hill's thick forests and cleared the land for construction. In 1883, Colonel Granville O. Haller, a Union Civil War veteran who'd been dismissed for disloyalty but was later exonerated, raised a towering mansion at Minor Avenue and James Street, which he called "Castlemount." More of the city's "first families" soon constructed pricey homes nearby, away from the hectic business district, turning First Hill into Seattle's first residential suburb. Among those following Haller's lead was German-born building contractor Otto Ranke. In the early 1890s he commissioned Elmer H. Fisher—the architect who'd rebuilt much of burned-out Pioneer Square—to create a three-story, turreted, Queen Anne–style residence for the Haller family near the corner of Terry Avenue and Marion Street (top, circa 1892). It was demolished in 1957.

The high-society habitués of First Hill enjoyed neighborhood traditions, including their annual Founders Day Ball. The first of these events was held on November 13, 1911, to commemorate the 60th anniversary of the landing of the Denny party pioneers at Alki Beach. Hosted by builder and contractor Morgan Carkeek and his wife, Emily, that initial ball was a costume party, with guests wearing attire appropriate to early Seattle. Guests were also asked to donate documents from the city's past along with other historical items. It was from the Founders Day Ball that the Seattle Historical Society was born, and the items the Carkeeks amassed became part of the collection now housed at the Museum of History and Industry (MOHAI). *Left:* A trio of flouncing ball goers in 1914.

Sorrento Hotel

In 1907, in preparation for the grand opening of Seattle's first world's fair, local clothier Samuel Rosenberg decided the city needed a compact new "family hotel," which he intended to call the Hotel Puget. But after buying two adjoining lots on First Hill and hiring architect Harlan Thomas, Rosenberg's dream expanded. The result was an L-shape, seven-story luxury inn, constructed in an eclectic Italianate style with a fireplace lounge, a roof garden, a formal courtyard, and top-floor dining facilities. The hotel (shown under construction at top left, circa 1908) was ultimately christened the Sorrento and opened just in time for fairgoers looking for suites equipped with private bathrooms. (U.S. President William Howard Taft was the first registered guest.) Unfortunately, the hotel was ahead of its time, and Rosenberg lost money before trading it for a 240-acre pear orchard near Medford, Oregon, where his sons, Harry and David Rosenberg, later built their mail-order fruit business, the profitable Harry & David. Over the decades, the Sorrento accommodated heavy loads of military personnel and served as the women's dormitory for a nearby college. In 1980, it was extensively refurbished by new owner and music industry executive Michael Malone. It's now considered one of the city's finest boutique hostelries (shown in the present-day photo at bottom left).

Summit School/The Northwest School

One of the first educational facilities to roll off the drawing board of Seattle School District architect James Stephen, Summit School was opened at the corner of Summit Avenue and Union Street in 1905, the year the above photograph was taken. An elegant wood-and-brick creation with decorative ironwork, it was closed as a public institution in 1965 but in 1980 reopened as The Northwest School, a private facility for middle- and high-school students. The building has been listed on the National Register of Historic Places since 1979 and is also a city of Seattle landmark.

St. James Cathedral

St. James Cathedral on First Hill is probably the best known Catholic church in Seattle, if only because it's easily spotted from the business district. It was commissioned by Bishop Edward J. O'Dea after he moved the See of the Nisqually Diocese from Vancouver, Washington, to Seattle in 1903. The architects were New Yorkers John L. Heins and Christopher G. LaFarge (designers of Manhattan's Cathedral of St. John the Divine and their city's earliest subway stations), who sent a pair of young associates—W. Marbury Somervell and Joseph S. Coté—to oversee the cathedral's construction. The Italian Renaissance Revival structure, with its 175-foot twin towers, was dedicated just before Christmas in 1907. In February 1916, the church's copper dome (shown on the left in the photograph at right) collapsed beneath 30,000 pounds of winter snow.

Left: In the aftermath of the collapse, the dome was replaced by a flat roof that lessened the cathedral's visual impact but is said to have improved interior acoustics.

Old King County Courthouse

In the early 1890s, the seat of judicial power in Seattle moved from what we now know as "Katzenjammer Castle," the city's first notable city hall on Third Avenue, to this pretentious edifice (left, circa 1908) at the southern end of First Hill. It was the first building in Washington to be designed by Willis A. Ritchie, an architect from the Midwest who would go on to create a number of county courthouses across the state, including those in Port Townsend, Olympia, and Spokane, all of which still stand. His pillared and domed King County Courthouse, located high above downtown (where Harborview Hospital now stands), was one of early Seattle's most familiar landmarks. It was also a target of derision. Lawyers were often heard cursing under their breaths as they panted up the steep incline from Pioneer Square to try cases or file actions at this courthouse, confirming a nickname for the knoll that had originally been bestowed by loggers: Profanity Hill. Ritchie's "cruel castle," as it was often called, was replaced in 1916 by a new courthouse on Third Avenue and was demolished in the 1930s.

Masonic Temple/ Egyptian Theatre

Members of the Freemasonry fraternal organization probably never imagined their temple on First Hill would one day become a center of popular culture, but that's exactly what has happened. Completed in 1915, this great brick block (right, circa 1916) at Harvard Avenue and East Pine Street was designed by Charles W. Saunders, who won the commission through a competition. It was originally a subdued sort of place, filled with offices and two auditoriums. But in the 1970s, the Masons hosted laserium shows and wrestling matches at the temple to raise money. By the 1980s, the building had been converted into a theater and became the home of the Seattle International Film Festival (SIFF). Its mix of Masonic symbols in stained glass with ersatz Egyptian décor can be jarring, but the structure remains one of this city's classiest movie houses. SIFF is still held here every spring.

CENTRAL DISTRICT

Cleared of its forests in the 1880s, what's now the Central District (or "CD"), east of the First Hill neighborhood, has gone through a succession of dominant populations. Originally the province of European farmers, the district evolved into a Jewish sector by 1900, with immigrants from Germany, Poland, and, later, the eastern Mediterranean opening synagogues, kosher markets, Hebrew schools, and coffee shops. During and after World War II, though, the CD began filling up with African American families who came here from the South to work for Boeing and other industries. Their settlement in this neighborhood built on an already rich history of black influence. In 1882, a wealthy black restaurateur and hotelier named William Grose purchased a 12-acre tract between what is now East Olive Street and East Madison Street at 24th Avenue and sold off lots to African American professionals and businessmen. Unfortunately, housing and job discrimination in the 20th century turned what many people hoped would be a prosperous black quarter into an area rife with racial tensions. Those strains only began to cool after the Seattle City Council passed an open housing law in 1968, and CD church leaders encouraged their congregations to combat poverty and lawlessness around them. Recently, many older African Americans have moved south to the Rainier Valley, and the restoration of historic homes has made the CD more attractive to young families of all colors. *Below:* Protestors against segregationist "Jim Crow laws" stand outside a grocery store on East Yesler Way in 1947.

New Providence Hospital, SEATTLE U.S.A.

Photo by F. H. Nol

Providence Hospital

From the 1870s until 1911, the Catholic order Sisters of Providence operated a hospital at Fifth Avenue and Spring Street in downtown Seattle (now the location of the U.S. Courthouse). That wood-frame structure had been designed by Mother Joseph, who came to the Pacific Northwest in the 1850s to establish hospitals, schools, and orphanages. The six-story brick structure that replaced her creation was opened in September 1911 at 17th Avenue and East Jefferson Street and was the work of architects W. Marbury Somervell and Joseph S. Coté, who'd previously worked on the St. James Cathedral on First Hill. The new hospital was a full-service facility boasting half a dozen operating rooms and a nursing school. It was served by a smokestack-bearing powerplant (seen above in this postcard, circa 1911). The Somervell-Coté edifice still stands, but its sale in 2000 to Seattle's Swedish Medical Center led to Providence Hospital being rechristened the Swedish Medical Center/Cherry Hill Campus. (Cherry Hill is the obscure name for the residential area of the Central District surrounding this health-care facility.)

Langston Hughes Performing Arts Center

Constructed between 1912 and 1915, the Synagogue of Chevra Bikur Cholim *(top, right)* was the work of theater architect B. Marcus Priteca. It was the second home of Seattle's earliest Jewish congregation, Bikur Cholim, and strongly resembles the Touro Synagogue in New Orleans, Louisiana. Located at 17th Avenue and East Yesler Way, this Byzantine-style structure was converted into a community center in the 1970s. It takes its present name from Langston Hughes, an African American poet, novelist, and playwright best known for his work during the Harlem Renaissance of the early 20th century. The synagogue-turned-theater *(bottom, right)* is listed in the National Registry as a historical landmark.

Birdland

As many thousands of African Americans moved to Seattle during the first half of the 20th century, they brought with them jazz, swing, and rhythm and blues to enliven the local music scene. Nightclubs opened along Jackson Street in Pioneer Square to host bands led by the likes of Lionel Hampton and Count Basie. Other venues took root in the Central District, one of the most memorable being Birdland at 22nd Avenue and East Madison Street (shown below, circa 1955). It began as the Savoy Ballroom and later became the Eastside Club, but in 1955 it reopened under new management as the Birdland Supper Club. The joint took its name from a much more famous establishment in New York City, which had been named in honor of jazz saxophonist Charlie "Bird" Parker. Seattle's Birdland booked such performers as Percy Mayfield, T-Bone Walker, Solomon Burke, James Brown, Jimi Hendrix, and Ray Charles. Eventually shedding its pretensions as a restaurant and staying open till 4 A.M., it became what one source called "probably *the* hottest after-hours dancehall in Seattle," drawing both black and white audiences. Around 1964, though, Birdland was finally closed—not due to lack of patronage but because a heavy snowstorm had shown the building to be structurally unsound.

CENTRAL LAKE SHORE

Before the advent of television, computer games, and social-networking sites, Seattle children spent warm summer days outside. They played baseball, rode bicycles along the cinder trails that crisscrossed this city in the early 20th century, or joined in water sports on the western shore of Lake Washington. In the mid-19th century, Henry Yesler did his best to denude the trees in the hills above that shoreline, but it wasn't until 1887—when J. M. Thompson inaugurated his Lake Washington Cable Railway between Pioneer Square and the tiny community of Leschi—that many people ventured out to see what the lakefront offered in terms of entertainment. At Leschi, Thompson and other entrepreneurs constructed a dance hall, a casino, a menagerie (with bears and other animals, which were eventually moved to Woodland Park Zoo), docks from which ferries could transport weekend sightseers to Mercer Island, and spacious bathing facilities. The photograph at right shows both men and women preparing at the Leschi boathouse for a 1925 swimming competition.

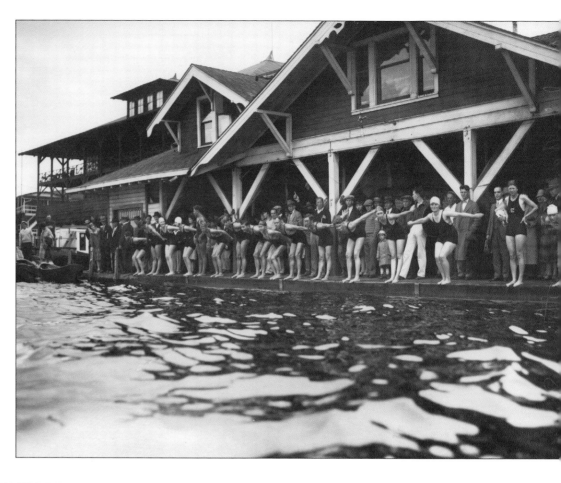

Thompson's cable car line (left, circa 1888) ran east along Yesler Way from Pioneer Square to Leschi, carrying pleasure-seekers out to shimmering Lake Washington in about 16 minutes. Returning to downtown, the open cars then traveled along Jackson Street. In 1889, buoyed by the success of that first railway, Thompson opened a second line out to Madison Park at the east end of Madison Street, where another amusement area already existed.

1743 A Scene in Denny-Blaine Park, Seattle, Washington.

Denny-Blaine Park

Spectacular views across Lake Washington toward the Cascade Mountains made the establishment of parks on that basin's west side almost inevitable. North of Leschi are Madrona Park and Denny-Blaine Park. The latter is a two-acre retreat that was donated to the city in the early 20th century by Charles L. Denny, son of Seattle founder Arthur Denny, and attorney Elbert F. Blaine, who had once served as Seattle parks commissioner. Both men purchased land north of Madrona with the idea of peddling it off to home builders, some of whom turned out to be the richest folks in Seattle. Among the Denny-Blaine neighborhood's historic homes are other pocket parks as well, one dedicated to Washington Territory's first governor, Isaac Stevens, another named for Charles Denny's wife, Viretta. *Left:* Denny-Blaine Park in 1914.

Madison Park

John J. McGilvra practiced law in Illinois before being tapped by President Abraham Lincoln in 1861 to become U.S. attorney for the Territory of Washington. Three years later, he settled in Seattle, purchased more than 400 acres of land on the west side of Lake Washington, and cut a straight road from downtown to his property (at his own expense), which became Madison Street (named for U.S. President James Madison). In the 1880s, McGilvra, now a judge, started platting and selling off his property, setting aside 24 acres for public use as Madison Park. Construction of the Madison Street Cable Car Company brought sightseers and picnickers to the area. Concerts were conducted on the moonlit waterfront, and in May 1890 the first professional baseball game in Seattle, pitting a local team against one from Spokane, was played there. Before long, Madison Park boasted a fancy boathouse, a wooden promenade, bandstands, a horse-racing track, and a small amusement park called White City. In 1922, Seattle acquired Madison Park and 20 years later initiated a Works Progress Administration (WPA) landscaping plan to improve the site. Most of Madison Park's historic facilities are long gone, but it remains popular with bikini-clad sunbathers and weekend strollers. *Right:* Canoeists swarm about a bathing pavilion at Madison Park, circa 1910.

CAPITOL HILL

Seattle High School (later renamed Broadway High School) was the first structure in this city designed specifically as an institution of secondary education. Opened in 1902, the Romanesque Revival–style building came from the drawing boards of William Boone, who had created the magnificent New York Block downtown, and his partner, James M. Corner. The institution functioned solely as a traditional high school until the Great Depression, when it added technical courses for out-of-work adults in need of new skills training. After World War II, Broadway High restricted its enrollment to returning veterans who wished to complete secondary school but didn't want to attend classes with children. In 1966, Seattle Community College purchased the edifice, and eight years later the building's two wings were demolished. Only the main structure was preserved. It is now Seattle Central Community College's Broadway Performance Hall. *Below:* Broadway High School is swarmed by teachers and students in 1909.

Bicycling Craze

The first bicycle was reportedly seen on Seattle's then unpaved streets in 1879. By 1896, the city claimed 300 two-wheeling men and women. To make up for a lack of decent local roads, a network of special bicycling tracks was created. One particularly popular route was along a cinder-covered trail (shown at right, circa 1901) that began at Eighth Avenue and Pine Street, in what were the far northern boondocks of downtown. From there, riders headed northeast along Lake Union, then east for about ten miles to Lake Washington. They passed over what's now tree-shaded Interlaken Boulevard at the north end of Capitol Hill; stopped for sandwiches, coffee, and gossip at a rustic halfway house located between Roanoke Park and 23rd Avenue; and finally crossed marshes and cable car tracks to Leschi.

R. D. Merrill House

To demonstrate both his wealth and taste, R. D. Merrill—the son of a distinguished lumbering dynasty from Michigan who had moved west in the late 1890s to manage his family's new holdings in Washington and British Columbia—commissioned Manhattan architect and landscape designer Charles A. Platt to create a residence for him at 919 Harvard Avenue East. Platt had a client list that ran heavy with Rockefellers, Roosevelts, and Astors, but he was equally recognized as the man responsible for the Freer Gallery of Art in Washington, D.C. (now part of the Smithsonian Institution). What he gave the lumber baron was a modified Georgian mansion, pushed up close to the street to allow room for an expansive, flat rear garden (shown at left, circa 1913). Helping Platt with that backyard's arrangement was Ellen Biddle Shipman, one of America's first female landscape architects. Her original plans for the property included a bowling green, a rose garden, a tennis court, and a vegetable garden. The R. D. Merrill House is listed in the National Register of Historic Places.

Fred Anhalt Apartments

Minnesota-born Frederick William Anhalt moved to the Puget Sound area in the early 20th century, intending to make his way as a butcher. Instead, he became the developer of some of this city's most distinctive apartment buildings. His early works were unremarkable, but as he taught himself more about classical European design, Anhalt's projects achieved greater distinction and elaboration. He was fond of adding turrets, leaded-glass windows, wood-paneled walls, individual fireplaces, terra-cotta embellishments, and lush landscaping. His units often featured both front and rear entrances. His development business went belly-up during the Great Depression, but Anhalt bought land near the University of Washington, which he turned into a prosperous nursery and sold to the university in 1973 for more than $1 million. Several of his apartment buildings still grace Capitol Hill. *Below:* The French Norman–style Fred Anhalt Apartments at 1005 East Roy Street, shown here in 1949, are now a city of Seattle landmark.

Millionaires' Row

While real-estate mogul James A. Moore wanted all of his Capitol Hill holdings to shine, he lavished particular attention on a once-gated stretch of 14th Avenue East directly south of Volunteer Park, nicknamed "Millionaires' Row." It was there that Moore erected a French Empire–style home for his own family. And there, too, that entrepreneur George H. Parker raised a Colonial Revival mansion in 1909 (seen on the lower right in this photograph, circa 1913). Parker made his fortune as chief sales agent in the West for the United Wireless Telegraph Company. That enterprise claimed to represent the expanding business interests of Guglielmo Marconi, chief developer of long-distance wireless telegraphy. However, in 1910, newspapers reported that United Wireless did not, in fact, represent Marconi's interests and that its many thousands of dollars worth of stock sales were fraudulent. Like other company executives, Parker was prosecuted and incarcerated. His mansion at 1409 East Prospect Street later became the residence of a Russian baron (supposedly an illegitimate son of Tsar Alexander II) and provided a setting for the 1988 Beau Bridges thriller *Seven Hours to Judgment*.

Right: The former home of George H. Parker, designed by architect Frederick Sexton, stands today as a reminder of Capitol Hill's former grandeur.

Samuel Hill Residence

Wealthy lawyer, financial manager, and "good roads" advocate Sam Hill was the Minneapolis, Minnesota-reared son-in-law of Great Northern Railway tycoon James J. Hill. In the 1890s, he became involved with gas and electric power businesses in Seattle and by the early 1900s had resettled in this city. To demonstrate his confidence in Seattle's future, Sam Hill commissioned Washington, D.C., architects Joseph Hornblower and J. Rush Marshall to design his family's new home at 814 East Highland Drive, in what's now the Harvard-Belmont Historic District. Hornblower & Marshall, who had created residences in the nation's capital and would

go on to plan what's now the Smithsonian Institution's National Museum of Natural History, gave Hill a concrete adaptation of an 18th-century manor house—one bearing a marked resemblance to Marie Antoinette's beloved Petit Trianon at Versailles, France. (The house is shown here in 1910 and is still standing today.) Hill would subsequently commission Hornblower & Marshall to create a slightly larger version of the house near Goldendale, in south-central Washington, overlooking the Columbia River. That building now houses the distinguished Maryhill Museum of Art.

Lake View Cemetery

Seattle's first municipal cemetery was located downtown near the present-day intersection of Denny Way and Dexter Avenue. In the 1880s, the city re-created that graveyard as a city park, moving the bodies to Capitol Hill. Unfortunately, the new burial ground was also later converted into a public commons—Volunteer Park—so the pioneers who'd been reinterred had to find a new final resting place, this time in Lake View Cemetery, immediately north of the park. No other cemetery in the city can claim better views or more celebrity "residents." Among those buried here are Seattle founding fathers David "Doc" Maynard, Henry Yesler, and Arthur Denny; Chief Sealth's daughter Princess Angeline; Madison Park creator John J. McGilvra; and early 20th-century sex-cult leader Franz Edmund Creffield. *Above:* Lake View's most visited grave marker may be that of martial arts film star Bruce Lee, a former Seattleite who is buried beside his son, Brandon Lee.

THE GREENING OF SEATTLE

BY 1900, SEATTLE HAD become rich from Klondike gold and busy with commercial and residential construction. However, its civic leaders acknowledged that it needed a comprehensive plan for growth and a strategy for the establishment of urban parks. So in 1903, the city council hired the prestigious Olmsted Brothers landscape architecture firm of Brookline, Massachusetts. John C. Olmsted *(inset)*, who with his stepbrother, Frederick Law Olmsted, Jr., had inherited the firm from Frederick Law Olmsted, Sr., the acclaimed father of American landscape design, came to Puget Sound to survey the town. Not long afterward, he submitted a plan outlining what the *Seattle Post-Intelligencer* called "a complete chain of parks and parkways, with playgrounds located at suitable points throughout the city."

Under John Olmsted's supervision, and using Seattle's powers of condemnation to acquire undeveloped property, a 20-mile belt of parklands and boulevards took shape, eventually reaching north and west from the Bailey Peninsula (rechristened Seward Park) on Lake Washington to Fort Lawton (today's Discovery Park) in Magnolia. Beacon Hill, Green Lake, Woodland, and Volunteer parks, as well as the Mount Baker neighborhood, were all eventually influenced by Olmsted's "City Beautiful" visions. So were Seattle's far northern reaches, where the Olmsted firm designed the lush Highlands subdivision for local business barons. The Olmsteds also created the site plan for the Alaska-Yukon-Pacific Exposition, held on the University of Washington grounds in 1909. Arguably, the 230-acre Washington Park Arboretum, planned in the 1930s and stretching south from Lake Washington's Union Bay, is the final jewel in the Olmsteds's necklace of parks.

Volunteer Park Water Tower

The Olmsteds's scheme for this park included the installation of some sort of observation tower. What the city built in 1906 was this husky, brick-faced water tower *(below)* at the corner of 14th Avenue and East Prospect Street on the park's southern edge. Visitors climb more than 100 steep interior steps for panoramic views of downtown, Puget Sound, and the distant snowy Olympic Mountain peaks. A standing exhibit on the observation level recounts the history and enduring legacy of Seattle's Olmsted parks plan.

VOLUNTEER PARK

In 1876, the city of Seattle purchased most of what's now 48-acre Volunteer Park near the center of Capitol Hill. However, it initially used part of that land as a graveyard and let the rest grow wild. In the late 1880s, caskets were moved to adjoining Lake View Cemetery, and the property was reserved as a place for "deep communion with nature." Following some minor landscape improvements, in 1901, the city council decided to rename the commons "Volunteer Park" in honor of the many Seattle men who had volunteered to fight in 1898's Spanish-American War. That same year, a 20-million-gallon public reservoir was scooped out of the park's southern flank to hold water piped in from the Cedar River, which runs westward from the Cascade Mountains to Lake Washington. However, the real work on Volunteer Park began after 1903, when the Olmsted Brothers's landscaping firm was hired to develop its comprehensive plan for Seattle's parks development. Second-growth fir trees were felled in favor of expansive lawns or more ornamental foliage. A sweeping concourse was created through the park, and play areas were developed. The photograph above (circa 1912) shows formal fountains and the reservoir on the left and a rustic music pavilion across the concourse to the right. The site's conservatory is visible in the distance.

Volunteer Park Conservatory

While the city relied on the Olmsteds for their expertise, it sometimes ignored their advice. Case in point: the installation in 1912 of an iron-framed conservatory at the park's north end. Patterned after Victorian England's monumental Crystal Palace exhibition hall, which was erected in London in 1851, this greenhouse was evidently selected from a catalog of prefabricated building plans and shipped west from New York, in pieces, to be assembled by Seattle park employees. The Olmsteds opposed its placement in Volunteer Park, but Capitol Hill burghers embraced the glass structure, contributing plant specimens to its collection. The statue outside its entrance is of William H. Seward, who, as U.S. secretary of state in 1867, negotiated America's acquisition of Alaska from Russia for two cents an acre. His bronze likeness is the work of New York artist Richard E. Brooks and was originally installed at Seattle's Alaska-Yukon-Pacific Exposition in 1909; it was moved here after the fair closed. Refurbished at great expense in the 1980s, the park's conservatory now welcomes more than a quarter of a million visitors annually to see its orchids, palms, cacti, and seasonal plants.

Seattle Asian Art Museum

The Olmsteds tolerated the addition of a water tower and conservatory to Volunteer Park. But in the 1920s, when Dr. Richard Fuller, president of the Seattle Fine Arts Society, proposed replacing the park's music pavilion with his new Art Institute, John Olmsted put his foot down. The city let Fuller go ahead anyway, which signaled the beginning of the end for the Olmsteds's involvement with Seattle. To design a home for the art collection he and his mother, Margaret MacTavish Fuller, had assembled over the decades, Fuller recruited Carl Gould, an École des Beaux-Arts alumnus who, with his longtime partner, Charles H. Bebb, had created buildings for the Government Locks at Ballard and Suzzallo Library at the University of Washington. Gould delivered to Fuller the first museum in America designed in the Art Moderne style—a sweeping, light-colored stone structure with a bravura interior garden court. That original Seattle Art Museum (SAM) was completed in 1933 (not long after the photo at right was taken). In 1991, SAM moved to new downtown digs (designed by Philadelphia architect Robert Venturi), and the Gould edifice was converted into the Seattle Asian Art Museum, displaying works from Japan, Korea, China, and elsewhere that had previously been in storage.

ARBORETUM/MONTLAKE

For decades, what's now the Washington Park Arboretum, between Capitol Hill and Madison Park, was owned by the Puget Mill Company and logged of its best timber. In 1900, the mill deeded 62 acres of that ravine-filled woodland to the city. The land was set aside as the new Washington Park, and acreage was added over the years. But other than the Olmsted brothers developing Lake Washington Boulevard and planning other meandering drives through the grounds, little was done to formalize the property's status as a public commons. Horse races were allowed on what's now Azalea Way, and the city dumped its garbage into the park's yawning ravines. Finally, in the 1930s, after the University of Washington agreed to help manage this land and establish a botanical garden on it, the Olmsteds were hired to create a master plan for the park. Thanks to labor provided by the Depression-era Works Progress Administration (WPA), clearing and planting got under way in earnest. Today, the Washington Park Arboretum comprises 230 acres, covered with some 20,000 trees, shrubs, and vines. Of the plants featured there, 139 varieties are endangered species. The grounds are open to the public year-round. *Below:* People stroll through the park in 1957.

Japanese Garden

Visions of creating a Japanese Garden in Seattle date to at least 1909 and the Alaska-Yukon-Pacific Exposition, but nothing happened for lack of funding. It took a large, anonymous donation to get things started in 1959. Today's tranquil, 3.5-acre garden in the Arboretum's southwest corner was originally created by Japanese landscape designer Juki Iida (but renovated in 2002 by Koichi Kobayashi). Construction included the transportation of 500 granite boulders from the Cascade Mountains, which were wrapped in bamboo matting to prevent damage. The garden's original teahouse, a gift from the city of Tokyo, was burned by vandals in 1973 and rebuilt in the '80s by Yasunori Sugita. The garden charges an entry fee and is closed from December through February. *Above:* Workers position a stone lantern near the teahouse in 1960.

Montlake Bridge

In 1925, eight years after the Lake Washington Ship Canal was completed, linking Puget Sound with Lake Union and Lake Washington, the Montlake Bridge was opened across that artificial waterway at 24th Avenue East. At least part of the impetus for the bridge's development was football. Work on the University of Washington Stadium, just north of this span, was completed in 1920, and soon afterward, Capitol Hill supporters of the Washington Huskies team began lobbying for a car-crossing at this point, which would be more convenient than having to drive all the way west to cross the Fremont Bridge. Today's Montlake Bridge is of a bascule design, anchored at either end by Neo-Gothic control towers created by architect Carl Gould, who wanted the towers to reflect the style of his buildings on the nearby UW campus.

Seattle Yacht Club

Seattle is a water-oriented city, so it should come as no surprise that it has its fair share of boating organizations. Among the most prominent is the Seattle Yacht Club (shown at left, circa 1925). Originally established in West Seattle in 1892, the Yacht Club moved to its present location on Portage Bay, just southwest of the Montlake Bridge, around 1921. Its Colonial Revival–style clubhouse was the work of architect John Graham, Sr., who was both a sailing enthusiast and a member of the organization. The Yacht Club now claims more than 3,000 members, and it traditionally sponsors the opening day of Seattle's boating season—an annual festival in May that began as long ago as 1913.

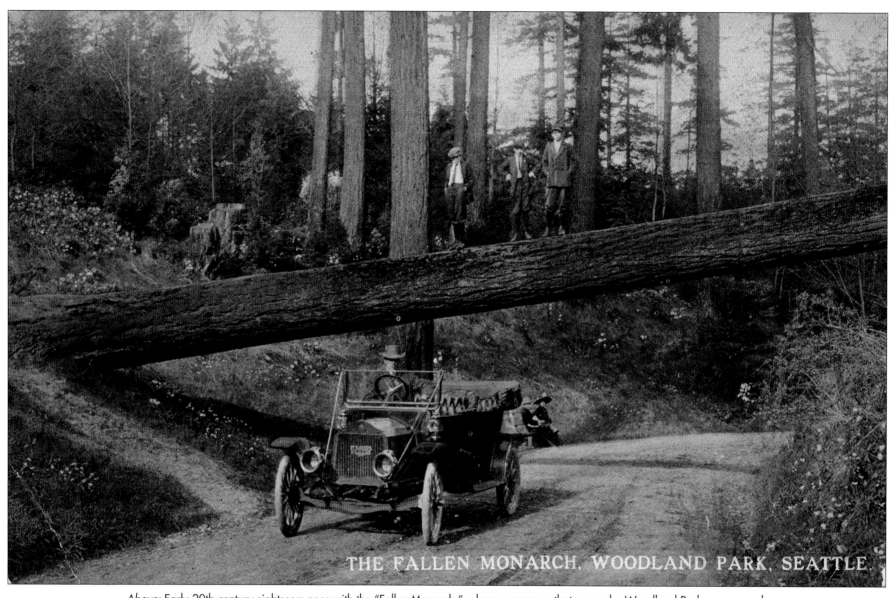

THE FALLEN MONARCH, WOODLAND PARK, SEATTLE.

Above: Early 20th-century sightseers pose with the "Fallen Monarch," a huge evergreen that crossed a Woodland Park access road.

THE MAGNETIC NORTH

It took Seattle two tries to become a properly incorporated town. The first municipal charter was issued by the Washington Territorial Legislature in January 1865, just four months before the end of America's bloody Civil War. A second and final charter was issued by the legislature in December 1869. Even then, though, Seattle wasn't as we know it today. It not only had a lot of growing up to do, but also a lot of growing *out*. By the time the Alaska-Yukon-Pacific Exposition took place in 1909, Seattle would be twice the size it had been during the Klondike Gold Rush.

GAINING GROUND

Seattle's dramatic expansion came through annexations of what had once been separate communities with their own mayors and city councils. Seattle initially covered a relatively small 12.67-square-mile area. But in 1891, the residents of Magnolia, Green Lake, Wallingford, and Brooklyn (today's University District) voted to turn their rival hamlets into Seattle neighborhoods, expanding the city to more than 29 square miles. An even bigger growth spurt came in 1907, when half a dozen additional towns—Southeast Seattle, Ravenna, South Park, Columbia City, Ballard, and West Seattle—all agreed to be annexed, many because they were having trouble acquiring ample water supplies and managing their own utilities. By the close of 1907, Seattle's borders encompassed 67.1 square miles. (Thanks to further annexations over the years, the city currently covers more than 91 square miles.)

INFRASTRUCTURE IMPROVEMENTS

As ribbons of new streetcar track were laid and new bridges were erected, formerly outlying communities no longer seemed as distant as they once had. That was particularly true of areas north of Lake Union and what's now the Lake Washington Ship Canal. Suddenly, it was not unheard of for a family to take a day trip out to Golden Gardens (north of Ballard) for a peaceful weekend stroll along the beach or to haul a picnic along to Guy Phinney's Woodland Park and visit some of the exotic animals he had on display. Subsequent road improvements and the great proliferation of automobiles after 1908 (the year mass-production of the Ford Model T began) made traveling between downtown and North Seattle communities commonplace.

What's remarkable is that any of the formerly independent towns swept into

Above: The Bar-B-Q Chuck Wagon (shown circa 1960) and other fast-food joints once catered to drivers along Aurora Avenue.

the city of Seattle during the late 1890s and early 1900s have retained a sense of individuality. But they have.

SCANDINAVIAN BALLARD

Take Ballard, for instance. Prior to the 1855 Point Elliott Treaty, which relocated most of the Native Americans who had been living around Puget Sound onto reservations, a tribe of Duwamish maintained encampments at both Salmon and Shilshole bays. That history, however, has long been forgotten. Instead, Ballard is now more familiarly distinguished by its Scandinavian character, a holdover from the early 20th century, when approximately 24,000 Swedes, Danes, Finns, and Norwegians lived in Seattle, many of them in Ballard. Census figures show that the number of Ballardites claiming Scandinavian heritage has dropped significantly in recent years, yet the district is still home to the largest Norwegian newspaper in America (the *Western Viking*), as well as to Seattle's Nordic Heritage Museum and the largest Sons of Norway club in the United States, where members continue to dine on pickled herring and egg sandwiches and other Scandinavian treats.

FUN IN FREMONT

Life is much different in Fremont. In place of Ballard's hardy, steadfast character, this neighborhood just to the east substitutes a wild-haired, iconoclastic independence. It didn't come as a surprise when Fremont declared itself one of the nation's first Nuclear-Free

Zones. And it's here that you'll find both a year-round, European-style Sunday street market and the annual Summer Solstice Parade and Pageant, an event renowned for its whopping puppets, garishly painted floats, and traditional armada of nude bicyclists. The fact that Fremont even continues to exist is sufficient reason to celebrate. The opening of the George Washington Memorial Bridge in 1932, which crossed the ship canal high above this district, and the discontinuation of north–south trolley service through Fremont in 1941 both dealt serious blows to the area. Economic downturns in Seattle during the 1960s and early '70s further threatened the future of this and other North Seattle communities. But in the '80s, Fremont was "rediscovered," and its historical architecture was rehabilitated for a whole new generation of residents, entrepreneurs, and artists.

ECCENTRIC AURORA AVENUE

Some parts of North Seattle haven't always demonstrated the highest standards of respectability. Aurora Avenue (old Highway 99)—once a six-lane introduction to family-owned motels and carhop-staffed drive-in eateries—has long been notorious for its population of sashaying prostitutes. The Coon Chicken Inn (part of a Utah restaurant chain), which did business from 1929 until 1955 at Lake City Way and 20th Avenue Northeast, probably marked the low point of local political correctness, with

Above: The Coon Chicken Inn

its entryway shaped like the grinning face of a black man wearing a porter's cap; diners entered through a big-lipped mouth.

HANGING' OUT

On the other hand, this quarter also hosts Green Lake, one of the city's foremost recreation spots, encircled by a wide path on which strollers, runners, and bicyclists have learned to coexist with a minimum of accidents. Adjacent to Green Lake is Woodland Park, with its eminent zoological gardens. And to the west are the Ballard Locks (officially the Hiram M. Chittenden Locks), built—like the rest of the Lake Washington Ship Canal—to handle immense oceangoing craft but mostly dealing with recreational vessels and the crowds that come out to watch them chug by on sunny summer afternoons.

Right: The annual Fremont Solstice Parade features elaborate costumes and floats.

BALLARD

Ballard owes its name to the outcome of a coin toss. The first land claim in the neighborhood was made in 1852, but it wasn't until 1882—when Judge Thomas Burke bought 720 acres of land north of Salmon Bay—that substantial acreage was platted there. Burke called his development Farmdale Homestead (intending to sell ten-acre plots to vegetable and fruit growers) and, along with his partners, set about creating a railroad connection with Seattle. Not long afterward, Captain William Rankin Ballard, who operated the sternwheeler *Zephyr* from Seattle south to Olympia, lost a coin toss and wound up in possession of 160 acres of dense timberland next to Farmdale as payment for a business debt. In 1888, Burke, Ballard, and others formed a joint improvement company and began selling off their subdivision—renamed Gilman Park—at a handsome profit. When the sector incorporated as a self-sufficient city in 1890, it adopted Captain Ballard's name. While it's now part of Seattle, Ballard retains a distinctive, small-town air that's reinforced by the character of Ballard Avenue, a four-block historic district crowded with brick, stone, and stucco commercial buildings dating from the late 19th and early 20th centuries. *Right:* Responding to an alarm, a speeding fire wagon turns onto Ballard Avenue from 20th Avenue Northwest, circa 1910.

Left: Today, historic Ballard Avenue is busy with restaurants, music venues, and distinctive small shops.

Old City Hall

In 1899, Ballard erected this distinguished City Hall (below, circa 1902) at 22nd Avenue Northwest and Ballard Avenue. Because it was still a small community, Ballard could fit its mayor's office, fire and police departments, *and* jail into the brick structure. It has often been said that Ballard managed to keep its peace by matching the number of saloon licenses it dispensed to the number of churches in town. However, no official records exist to prove or disprove such an arrangement. When Ballard was annexed to Seattle in May 1907—a move made in the hopes of improving its water supply—City Hall was supposedly draped in black crepe, and its flag was lowered to half-mast while the bell in its tower tolled mournfully. Clearly, Ballard's citizens were not happy about the change. This edifice stood until 1967, when it was demolished following severe earthquake damage. The site is now a compact park called Marvin's Garden, dedicated to Marvin Sjoberg, a local character who, during much of the 20th century, styled himself as Ballard's "unofficial mayor." A squat brick tower in the park holds the old City Hall's original brass bell.

Shingle Capital of the World

While it's hard to imagine now, the skies above Ballard were once murky with smoke from this district's many sawmills and shingle mills. The first shingle mill was established in 1888, and it turned the Pacific Northwest's then plentiful tall timber into building materials. By 1895, Ballard touted itself as the "Shingle Capital of the World." Of the Seattle area's 31 shingle mills, a third was located in Ballard; these facilities employed almost 600 men. It was said that Ballard produced more shingles than any other town on the planet. Its success was due in part to the Great Fire of 1889, which had reduced Seattle's downtown and milling facilities to ashes. Much of the lumber used to rebuild Seattle came from Ballard. By 1904, Ballard laid claim to 20 mills, including the prominent Stimson Mill (shown above, circa 1910). The waterfront was thick with bobbing log booms. Three million shingles were being turned out in Ballard mills every day by men who worked ten-hour shifts, seven days a week.

Left: Ballard's fishing fleet caught tons of salmon every year. The fish were cleaned by the men and then packed by women at Washington canneries such as this one, shown circa 1946.

Golden Gardens Park

At the north end of Shilshole Bay is 87-acre Golden Gardens Park. It's popular now with beachcombers and windsurfers, but a century ago Ballardites camped there during sweltering summer nights hoping to catch cool breezes off Puget Sound. The park was established by Harry Whitney Treat, a Wisconsin-born Harvard Law graduate who had prospered at real-estate speculation. He arrived in Seattle during the first years of the 20th century, constructed a 17,000-square-foot mansion (now a historic landmark) on Queen Anne's Highland Drive, and began buying forested and waterfront acreage in Seattle's northwest corner. He named his most prominent residential development, located just east of Golden Gardens, Loyal Heights after his youngest daughter, Loyal Graef Treat. To goad sales, Treat rolled an electric trolley line out to his remote properties and created a small amusement park at Golden Gardens. He hoped that townsfolk who visited the beach there for a weekend swim or picnic could also be persuaded to buy his adjacent home sites. Treat was killed in a 1922 car accident, and the city purchased Golden Gardens from his estate. Half a decade later, it was opened as a municipal park. *Right:* Golden Gardens beach, circa 1928.

Left: Although the beach remains the focus at Golden Gardens, the park today also offers hikes through the adjacent forest and an off-leash area for dogs.

Lake Washington Ship Canal

Talk of an artificial canal connecting freshwater Lake Washington with saltwater Puget Sound probably began with Thomas Mercer. In 1854, confident that such a passage would someday be dug, Mercer named the giant body of water that lay between them "Lake Union." Early, private attempts to create such a course for boats and the transportation of logs were only minimally successful. Rival proposals considered other options: enlarging the Black River, which ran from the south end of Lake Washington to the Duwamish River; excavating a waterway from Lake Washington through the Rainier Valley to the mouth of the Duwamish; or creating a channel from the south end of Lake Union through what's now Lower Queen Anne to Smith Cove on Elliott Bay. In 1910, Major Hiram M. Chittenden, local district manager for the Army Corps of Engineers, won congressional approval to construct a massive locks system between Shilshole and Salmon bays in Ballard and remove an isthmus at Montlake that separated Lakes Union and Washington. In 1911, work began to dig a conduit wide enough and deep enough to carry warships. The eight-mile-long Lake Washington Ship Canal was finally opened on July 4, 1917. *Left:* Construction of the canal locks in 1913.

Hiram M. Chittenden Locks

Because the levels of Puget Sound and Lake Washington were originally different, opening the canal resulted in the lake's water level being lowered by nine feet. The two-lock system (one for small boats, the other for larger craft) now maintains a steady water level in Lakes Union and Washington. For many years after their dedication, the area around the locks—which had been quite torn up during construction—remained rather barren-looking. Architect Carl Gould, who designed the adjacent buildings, also inked out a plan for landscaping. But it wasn't until 1931, when the Corps of Engineers hired a young botanist from southwest Washington State, Carl S. English, Jr., that the gardens there really began to take shape and draw public attention, as English added plantings from around the world. Visitors to what are now the Hiram M. Chittenden Locks *(right)*—renamed in their creator's honor in 1956—are invited to picnic among English's seven acres of lawn, trees, and flowers. There's also a fish ladder there, opened in 1976. In excess of half a million salmon, steelhead, and trout negotiate that ladder every year, bound for spawning areas in the Cascade Mountains.

FREMONT

Few Seattle neighborhoods possess reputations quite as distinct—or quirky—as Fremont. Located in the northwest corner of Lake Union, on the north side of the Lake Washington Ship Canal, this hub of historical residences, high-tech companies, and playful public art was platted in 1888 by developers Edward Blewett and Luther H. Griffith. Investing with them in this independent suburb was dentist and electric power promoter Edward Corliss Kilbourne, who hailed from Aurora, Illinois. This trio hoped to take advantage of a new lumber mill that had been established near their town site and of the fact that the primeval woodlands north of Seattle had recently become more accessible via a railroad spur. Three years

after they began peddling lots in the hamlet they named Fremont (after Blewett and Griffith's Nebraska hometown; Kilbourne got to name what would become North Seattle's main thoroughfare, Aurora Avenue), their faith was rewarded: The district had grown to 5,000 residents and was annexed by Seattle. As transportation advances over the decades turned north-of-the-canal quarters into easily reachable bedroom communities, Fremont evolved from being the pipe dream of midwestern transplants to what its residents now like to call it: "the Center of the Universe." *Bottom, left:* Fremont Avenue looking north from North 34th Street, circa 1935.

People Waiting for the Interurban

A century ago, interurban trains rattled through Fremont, carrying passengers as far north as Everett and south to Tacoma. The train service was discontinued in 1939, seven years after Highway 99/Aurora Avenue was completed. The only reminder of that mass-transit system is a popular sculpture at the intersection of Fremont Avenue and North 34th Street. Created by Washington artist Richard Beyer, *People Waiting for the Interurban* was installed in 1978. It features five people standing beneath a pergola in anticipation of the train's approach. Glimpsed between their legs is a dog with a human face, said to be the visage of Arman Napoleon Stepanian, a curbside-recycling advocate known in the late 20th century as the unofficial "mayor of Fremont." Fremonsters (yes, that's really the nickname for this neighborhood's residents) like to have fun with Beyer's iconic sculpture, dressing its people for special occasions and different seasons.

Fremont Drug Company

This two-story, wood-framed structure is the oldest building still standing in Fremont. It was constructed in the early 1890s on the south side of what's now the Lake Washington Ship Canal. However, by 1895 it had been moved by a team of oxen to the northwest corner of Fremont Avenue and Ewing Street (now North 34th Street), where it housed the Fremont Drug Company, shown at left, circa 1907. As early as 1901, the neighborhood's first public library was established on this building's second floor. By the 1930s, the building was occupied by the Fremont Tavern, which in the 1980s was transformed into the more upscale Red Door Ale House. In 2001, the structure was relocated once more—lock, stock, and beer barrels—this time one block west to Evanston Avenue, to make room for a retail and housing complex.

Right: Where simple lunch counters and taverns once dominated the intersection of Fremont and 34th, there are now upscale coffee shops and ethnic eateries.

B. F. Day Elementary School

Said to be the oldest continuously operating elementary institution in the Seattle School District, B. F. Day (which offers kindergarten through fifth grade) opened in Fremont in the fall of 1892. The land on which it stands was given to the city by Benjamin Franklin Day and Francis Day, who operated a 160-acre farm on the edge of Fremont. They donated the property (originally valued at $10,000) to ensure the establishment of a proper school in their community; for many years previous, children were taught their lessons in private homes. The original brick B. F. Day building contained four rooms and was designed by the school district's first resident architect, John Parkinson. In 1901, an eight-room addition, created by the district's latest designer, James Stephen, and adhering to Parkinson's original style, was constructed. (The photo at right shows the expanded edifice in 1902.) For much of the early 20th century, B. F. Day, located at 3921 Linden Avenue North, claimed to be the largest elementary school in Seattle, with 900 students enrolled in the mid-1920s. Further additions in 1916 were made to accommodate them all. This historic landmark underwent a multimillion-dollar renovation in the 1990s.

Corliss P. Stone Residence

After moving from Vermont to Seattle in 1861, Corliss P. Stone built prosperous grocery and real-estate businesses, served on the city council, and constructed this home near the intersection of North 35th Street and Woodland Park Avenue North. In 1872, Republican Stone (the uncle of Fremont cofounder Edward C. Kilbourne) was elected as Seattle's third mayor. But just seven months later, he absconded to San Francisco with $15,000 taken from his merchandising partnership with Charles H. Burnett. As Seattle's *Weekly Intelligencer* reported, that money was to have been used in "making payment to creditors." However, Corliss apparently changed his mind, informing Burnett that he'd appropriated the cash "to my private use" and was leaving for the East, having "abandoned all idea of continuing his business here." Records aren't clear on how Stone redeemed himself, but he must have done so, since when he died in 1906—back once more in Seattle—he was hailed as a prominent capitalist.

Fremont Troll

Whimsical. That's the adjective best applied to Fremont's public artwork. In addition to *People Waiting for the Interurban*, there's a 53-foot Cold War–era rocket fuselage that used to be attached to a Belltown surplus store and now hangs from a building at Evanston Avenue North and North 35th Street. A 16-foot-tall bronze likeness of former communist leader Vladimir Lenin looms above the corner of Evanston and 36th Street. And a troll peeks out from beneath the north end of the Aurora Bridge *(right).* Yes, a bent-nosed, bug-eyed, long-locked troll. It looks like an escapee from a Brothers Grimm nightmare, only this troll is 18 feet tall, made of ferroconcrete, and squeezes a real Volkswagen Bug in its left hand. Constructed in 1990, the troll is a collective project created under the auspices of the Fremont Arts Council. It is now the gathering place every October for a song, dance, and circus celebration called Trolloween.

Late for the Interurban

Folks who grew up in the Puget Sound area between 1958 and 1981 were likely "Patches Pals" at one time. That is, they were faithful watchers of the *J. P. Patches Show,* a popular, twice-daily, locally produced program for children. It featured a screwball clown known as Julius Pierpont "J. P." Patches (played by Chris Wedes) as the "Mayor of the City Dump," and Gertrude, his red-mop-wigged, suspiciously masculine girlfriend (played by Bob Newman, who also portrayed just about every other supporting member of the cast). The show both entertained and sought to instill good habits in its young viewers. To celebrate the 50th anniversary of that iconic TV program, this statue *(left)*—created by sculptor Kevin Pettelle and showing J. P. and Gertrude in a familiar can't-decide-which-way-to-go arm lock—was installed in Fremont's Solstice Plaza in 2008, at Fremont Avenue North and North 34th Street. In tribute to Richard Beyer's better-known Fremont artwork, Pettelle's sculpture is called *Late for the Interurban.*

AURORA AVENUE

Horse-drawn wagons and streetcars opened North Seattle as a residential district, but it was the automobile that really accelerated this city's northward expansion. The construction of Highway 99, running up the West Coast from California to Blaine, Washington, on the Canadian border, took place mostly during the 1920s and '30s. That roadway, also known as Aurora Avenue and the "Blue Star Memorial Highway" (a post–World War II tribute to U.S. soldiers) eased long-distance travel but also incited business development along its Seattle corridor. Important to the avenue's completion was the opening in 1932 of the George Washington Memorial Bridge—better known as the Aurora Bridge—which vaults across Lake Union between the Fremont and Queen Anne neighborhoods. A graceful 2,945-foot steel cantilever span, the bridge was created by the Seattle engineering firm Jacobs and Ober. Once fairly quiet, the viaduct is now heavily trafficked by impatient commuters. It is also the last stop for many disconsolate Seattleites. The first suicide jumper was a salesman who leapt to his death before the span was even finished; since then, an average of three to four have taken the plunge annually, though some have actually survived the fall.

Twin Teepees Restaurant

As more and more people traveled by automobile during the early 20th century, roadside businesses sprang up to service them. Many of these enterprises, especially restaurants, did whatever they could to draw attention. The Twin T-P's (later rechristened Twin Teepees) was a prime example of this "vernacular architecture." Opened on the west side of Green Lake in 1937, the restaurant featured a pair of metal-clad conical pavilions connected by a passageway. The dining room was located in one of these ersatz tents, while the other contained the kitchen and a cocktail lounge. The mishmash of Native American motifs drew many a photographer. Outside, the restaurant resembled giant Plains Indian teepees, while inside the ceilings were covered with Northwest Coast Indian designs. As the decades went on, the exterior was painted with stripes to look even more like cloth, but the food stayed the same—American cuisine, heavy on the steak and chicken. Unfortunately, fires in 1997 and 2000 were the death of the Twin Teepees. Much to the dismay of historical preservationists, the restaurant was demolished in 2001.

The Twin Teepees was hardly the only curious bit of kitsch put up during the 20th century to draw the eyes of Aurora Avenue drivers. Between the Aurora Bridge and 145th Street in North Seattle, motorists encountered a bigger-than-life-size seal with a ball balanced on its nose outside a motel; an elaborate blue-whiskered neon rabbit advertising Harvey's Tavern; a life-size replica of an Indian elephant *(inset)*, complete with maharajah's seat (created in the 1930s by a mosaic artist and poised outside a flower shop); a Moorish-style Arabian Theater (shown at left, circa 1932), fronted by colorful tile and glasswork, which has since been converted from a movie palace into a church; and other assorted tacky treasures of the silly or salacious variety.

GREEN LAKE

The original name of North Seattle's immense glacier-created reservoir (shown at right, circa 1900) was "Lake Green." This name was bestowed upon the lake in the mid-1850s by a U.S. government surveyor astounded by its prolific algae blooms. The first to claim adjacent land was Erhart "Green Lake John" Siegfried, a German immigrant who in 1869 staked out 130 acres and built a log cabin at the basin's north end. By the 1880s, developers such as Guy Phinney and William D. Wood were clear-cutting the surrounding acreage for "suburban" home-lot sales. However, Wood—who would eventually be elected mayor of Seattle—also encouraged lawmakers to preserve the lakefront. "No other city in the Union," he wrote, "has within its limits such a symmetrical and available frontage for public recreation and enjoyment of natural beauty...." The Olmsted brothers agreed. As part of their 1903 comprehensive plan, they recommended that the city purchase Green Lake, block its inflow, and lower its level by seven feet in order to expose hundreds of acres of land for parks development and the creation of an encircling boulevard. This was accomplished in 1911; the downside was that cutting off the natural flow of water eventually led to a decades-long fight against algae growth. Nonetheless, Green Lake is today one of Seattle's premier retreats.

There have been few times since the 1940s that enough ice has formed atop Green Lake to permit winter recreation on its surface. But during the late 19th and early 20th centuries, ice-skating was popular there. In particularly chilly weather, neighborhood residents would raise bonfires along the shore, gather to hear amateur musicians, clamp ice skates onto their shoes with the help of tightening keys, and slide out onto the surface hand in hand with parents or prospective mates. Less frequent wintertime pursuits included dog sledding on Green Lake. The photo at left shows champion musher Wayne Goyne and his anxious team ready to tackle the frozen lake in December 1919.

Aqua Follies

Beginning in August 1950, Green Lake hosted one of the summer season's foremost attractions: a combination of water ballet, comedy, and other amusements known as the Aqua Follies. These took place at the Aqua Theater, which combined a performance pool, twin diving platforms, and seating for 5,200 people at the lake's south end. Held in conjunction with Seattle's annual summer Seafair celebration, the Aqua Follies featured female synchronized swimmers (the Aqua Dears, shown at left in 1961), stage dancers (the Aqua Darlings), and assorted stunt divers of both genders. The Aqua Theater is also remembered for its jazz and orchestral performances, musicals, and fireworks displays. Its heyday came during the 1962 World's Fair, when so many tourists were in town. But its decline followed quickly, as Seattleites eventually turned to the indoor venues at Seattle Center for their entertainment. The Aqua Follies ended in 1964, and their lakeside theater was dismantled. What remains is a much smaller grandstand.

Green Lake Public Library

Although the lake draws the most attention to this bustling neighborhood, it is surrounded by some grand homes, many small businesses, and a few historic structures. Most notable in that last category is one of Seattle's finest small branch libraries, at the corner of East Green Lake Drive North and 4th Avenue Northeast. The Green Lake Public Library—shown at right in 1931—was among several local book repositories given to the city a century ago by steel magnate Andrew Carnegie. (Other Carnegie branch libraries can be found in Fremont, Ballard, the University District, Queen Anne, and West Seattle.) Designed in a modern French Renaissance style by W. Marbury Somervell and Joseph S. Coté, the library opened in 1910 and is now listed on the National Register of Historic Places.

WOODLAND PARK

Guy Carleton Phinney was a flamboyant Scotsman from Nova Scotia, Canada, who had made a fortune in real estate and lumber mill investments before reaching Seattle. In the late 1880s, he purchased about 340 acres of land on a high ridge west of Green Lake. There he built his family a scenic estate, "Woodland Park," complete with a mansion, English-style gardens, and a menagerie. He also laid a streetcar line north from Fremont to his new home. He hoped to draw Seattleites from downtown, show them the beauty of what's now Phinney Ridge, and then sell them parts of his holdings. As more and more people came, he constructed a hotel and a conservatory and added African ostriches to the bear, deer, and other animals in his zoo. Unfortunately, Phinney died in 1893 at age 41, and his widow, Nellie, was forced to sell their property to the city of Seattle in 1899. *Top, left:* Woodland Park, looking south toward Fremont from Phinney's hotel, in 1891.

Woodland Park Zoo

In 1904, the city opened Woodland Park Zoo (right, circa 1915). It included not only Phinney's private menagerie, but also animals that had previously been exhibited among the entertainments at Leschi Park. As part of their comprehensive planning for Seattle, the Olmsted brothers made a number of changes to this zoo, expanding its exhibit areas and creating cramped quarters for bears and other formerly wild inhabitants. Most of the animals lived in barren cages with concrete floors, and visitors could stroll right up to the enclosures and toss food into the jaws of whatever lived inside. Over the next half-century, outside pens were built (for elk and bison); increasingly exotic animals were brought to Woodland Park (sea lions, coatimundi, polar bears, elephants, kangaroos); and inhumane quarters were slowly replaced with slightly more natural habitats.

The Zoo Today

By the 1970s, Woodland Park Zoo was in need of a large-scale and pricey overhaul. A new master plan was developed, with the intention of presenting animals and birds in more spacious facilities reminiscent of their native habitats. Today's 92-acre facility *(right)* features an award-winning Tropical Rain Forest exhibit; an Asian elephant forest; a Northern Trail exhibit, emulating an actual track through Alaska's Denali National Park; an African Savanna, where hippopotami and giraffes roam with some degree of freedom; and a Temperate Forest with more than 50 different kinds of birds. In addition, the zoo grounds host summer concerts and plays, as well as a hand-carved wooden carousel (circa 1918) that had originally been installed at the Cincinnati Zoo.

Stars Behind Bars

Left, top: Tusko was a ten-foot Asian elephant, shipped to the United States from Thailand in 1898. After being exhibited in circuses and at an Oregon amusement park and earning a reputation for cantankerousness (as well as drunkenness), Tusko was brought to Seattle in chains on a flatbed truck in 1932 and displayed by a sideshow huckster. Appalled, Mayor John F. Dore ordered the pachyderm confiscated and transferred to Woodland Park Zoo. At least initially, children donated their pennies to feed Tusko. He remained at the zoo until his death in 1933. *Left, bottom:* Bobo the Gorilla came to America as an infant from Africa in 1951 and wound up living with a family in Anacortes, north of Seattle. Even before he turned two, though, Bobo had outgrown his human home and was taken to Woodland Park Zoo. Bobo could be grumpy and aggressive, and he managed to frustrate zookeepers by fending off the romantic advances of a female gorilla, Fifi. Yet he won the hearts of a generation of local schoolchildren. After he died in 1968, Bobo was stuffed and put on display at the Museum of History and Industry (MOHAI) in Montlake, where he still remains.

STAY BACK OF RAILING
DONT TOUCH OR TAP ON

GREENWOOD

Originally called Woodland, the Greenwood neighborhood—east of Ballard and northwest of Green Lake—was for many years dismissed as too marshy and forested for cost-effective development. As late as 1900, there were still far more evergreen trees there than residents. Part of the reason may be that much of the area had been designated as the site of a mammoth cemetery, though there were never many graves dug. What's now the busy intersection of Greenwood Avenue and North 85th Street was notably quiet at the turn of the last century *(left)*, with little more than a couple of grocery stores, a real-estate office, a feed store, and a dirt-

and-plank buggy road leading north to Edmonds. In 1907, though, the cemetery property was sold and platted for residential and commercial construction as the Greenwood Addition. Although a streetcar line had been laid from Fremont to what's now Woodland Park in 1890, it was mostly used by weekend sightseers. It wasn't until the opening in 1910 of electric interurban rail service from Seattle to Everett, with stops in Greenwood, that this neighborhood finally became easily accessible and began to attract residents in great numbers.

Greenwood Elementary School

Many of the elementary-education buildings architect James Stephen created in the first years of the 20th century were made of wood. They often had identical floor plans, though their exterior elevations and embellishments varied. The raising of those structures was done quickly, satisfying a long-standing need for more and better schools. But after a 1907 trip to study educational facilities in the Midwest and New York, Stephen developed a second model plan for local grade schools, using fireproof materials—brick, terra-cotta, and concrete—in place of wood. This model called for nine classrooms on two floors, steeply pitched roofs, and facades executed in Jacobean style, an amalgam of Tudor and Elizabethan modes that was much in vogue then. Greenwood Elementary School (shown at top, circa 1922 and at bottom in present day) was built in 1909 on Northwest 80th Street, is one of the finest remaining examples of that model. It was renovated and modernized in 2002.

Located at Greenwood Avenue and North 78th Street, the Ridgemont Theater *(left)* opened in 1923. It was popular for its brick and stucco facade as well as its Kimball organ, which was played for many years by noted musician Ed Zollman. That organ was later moved to a church in Snohomish, while the theater—"modernized" by ugly exterior panels that concealed its elegant detailing—began running foreign and "art" films in the 1960s, one of the first local movie houses in the area to do so. Closed in 1989, the theater was torn down 12 years later. An undistinguished, 21-condominium building, also called The Ridgemont, now stands in its place.

A STYLE WORTH SAVING

GIVEN SEATTLE'S FREQUENTLY drippy weather, it is easy to understand why bungalow-style residences—with their gabled roofs, deep eaves, and roomy covered front porches—became very popular here in the late 19th and early 20th centuries. Usually one story in height, they were ideal for small lots, fit in well with the area's natural environment, and made use of locally available materials: lumber for general construction and stone for the fireplaces that, like built-in bookshelves, were innovations indicative of this style. Perhaps best of all, bungalows, with their clean and simple lines, were relatively inexpensive to build. Plans and specifications were made available through widely distributed magazines, such as Gustav Stickley's *The Craftsman* and *Bungalow Magazine*, a Seattle-produced publication linked to a company that once raised and sold bungalow homes on the installment purchase plan. Contractors and tract developers put up thousands of these single-family dwellings all over the Pacific Northwest. But during the 1990s and early 21st century, as property values shot up in Seattle, many were either demolished in favor of more spacious homes or were enlarged and thus disfigured. As bungalows have disappeared, they have become "the new spotted owl of the urban ecosystem," according to *Seattle Weekly*.

The A.Y.P. Exposition from Captive Balloon A Quarter of a Mile Above the Earth.

X 4000

Copyright, 1909
by
F.H.Nowell

FAIR ENOUGH

In 1909, two decades after its phoenixlike rebirth and in the midst of a building and population boom, Seattle threw itself a party: Washington's first world's fair. The intent was at least twofold: to focus public attention and money on this drizzly corner of the Pacific Northwest and to show up rival Portland, Oregon, which had staged an extravagant Lewis and Clark Centennial Exposition in 1905. During its slightly more than half-century history, Seattle had overcome its backwoods bumpkinhood to emerge as a major player in Pacific Rim trade. City fathers didn't think it possible to overstate their pride in that hard-won prominence.

Edmond S. Meany, a onetime state legislator and professor at the University of Washington, proposed mounting the Seattle fair on the UW campus, which remained largely vacant ten years after that institution relocated to the north shore of Portage Bay. Organizers agreed—even though hosting the fair there would mean it had to be non-alcoholic, since state law forbade liquor on the campus grounds. An organizing committee was assembled, funds were raised, and San Francisco architects John Galen Howard and John Debo Galloway were engaged to plan the site.

THE A-Y-P

The resulting Alaska-Yukon-Pacific Exposition proved as enlightening as it was entertaining. States such as California, Oregon, New York, and Alaska erected gaudy pavilions on the grounds.

Other structures celebrated U.S. mining, manufacturing, and forestry, as well as the fine arts. While fair planners had hoped the expo would draw more international participation than it ultimately did, at least Sweden, Japan, and Canada contributed exhibit buildings to the site. Those last two pavilions, together with the Hawaii Building, justified the "Pacific" part of this exposition's protracted moniker. Visitors who tired of educational presentations could stroll across to the Pay Streak amusement zone or pay $1 to climb high above the fair in the basket of a helium balloon. There was so much fun to be had for so little. According to the *Seattle Post-Intelligencer*'s calculations, someone partaking of every one of this expo's paid attractions would have to plunk down only $15.20 (not including the costs for food and souvenirs). Yet, up to 2,000 people

Above: David Stern, owner of a Seattle advertising agency, lays claim to the creation of the famed Smiley Face symbol.

Left: An aerial view of the 1909 Alaska-Yukon-Pacific Exposition taken from a balloon

evaded the fifty-cent admission fee to the fairgrounds by sneaking in through an unguarded, quarter-mile-long sewer tunnel. It took a week for officials to figure out why so many visitors had "muddy shoulders"—the result of squeezing through the manholes at either end.

Although Seattle benefited from the tourist dollars brought in by the Alaska-Yukon-Pacific Exposition, hopes that the fair would boost trade were not realized. Nonetheless, it did leave behind several structures that remain in use at the UW, including the Fine Arts Palace (now Architecture Hall), the Women's Building (today's Cunningham Hall), and Drumheller Fountain, from which Mount Rainier can be spotted on clear days.

NEIGHBORHOOD TENSIONS

In the century since that first world's fair, the UW (pronounced "U Dub") and the residential-commercial district surrounding it have grown immensely—but not always peacefully. From 1947 through 1948, both fell under the scrutiny of an anticommunist crusader named Albert F. Canwell. A first-term Republican state legislator from Spokane, Canwell was convinced that Washington—and especially its premier university—was a hotbed of anti-American radicalism. Presaging U.S. Senator Joseph McCarthy's later "red scare" persecutions, Canwell sought to expose the "probably not less than 150" UW faculty members he believed were "Communists or sympathizers of the Communist party." Eschewing conventional rules of cross-

examination and admissible evidence, Canwell held hearings that destroyed reputations and led to the dismissal of three faculty members before voters finally booted him from office.

Two decades later, the University District endured further tension when national student unrest led to numerous antiwar and antisegregation protests here. While such activism didn't provoke extraordinary violence in Seattle, it did supposedly lead to the invention of the Happy Face (or Smiley Face). David Stern, who in the 1960s operated a local advertising agency, is one of several people credited with creating that lemon-yellow symbol of peace and emotional uplift, which Stern originally stamped on buttons handed out by a University District savings and loan in 1966.

CALMER QUARTERS

The two neighborhoods immediately adjacent to this district on the west and north—Wallingford and Ravenna, respectively—have enjoyed more serene histories.

Wallingford was once known for its dairies, later for the soot-and spark-spewing Seattle Gas Company plant on its Lake Union waterfront (highlighted in Chapter 3). Today, it's a showcase of classic bungalow homes and a haven for young singles. The main commercial thoroughfare through Wallingford is North 45th Street, with its abundance of restaurants, fewer but nonetheless prominent movie theaters, and crowded parking conditions. (Don't hold out much hope of

finding a free spot just off 45th either; Wallingforders may seem like laid-back sorts, but they've been adamant about restricting public parking outside their homes.)

Ravenna, meanwhile, takes its name from a northern Italian city known for its canals and Christian monuments. But Seattle's Ravenna is more noteworthy for its parks. During the 1909 World's Fair, field trips to the "Big Trees of Ravenna

Above: Ravenna Park is a quiet sanctuary for Seattle families.

Park" were popular with tourists, and brochures promoted the neighborhood as "Nature's Exposition." Sadly, many of its largest evergreens have long since disappeared. Ravenna has become a destination for woodland lovers who still look to Ravenna Park and adjoining Cowen Park for essential escapes from the frenetic metropolis Seattle leaders of 100 years ago were so anxious to build.

Right: Protestors outside the Canwell committee hearings, 1968

WALLINGFORD

When providing directions to Wallingford, modern Seattleites generally say it's east of Fremont and west of the University District. But a century ago, the area, which was known as Interlake, was described as being between Lake Union on the south and Green Lake on the north. Wallingford acquired its present moniker from John Noble Wallingford, a real-estate developer who came to Seattle from Maine in 1888. He purchased and platted as much land as he could in this quarter, which by then had already been denuded of its old-growth timber. The stitching of electric trolley lines through this vicinity spurred the birth of small, separate communities, such as Edgewater and Latona, which—like Wallingford—were annexed to Seattle in 1891 and have since been embraced within this neighborhood's boundaries. Wallingford Center, a three-story, neoclassical wooden behemoth (shown at right, circa 1911) serves as a reminder of the district's roots. It's now a mixed-use retail and residential complex at Wallingford Avenue North and North 45th Street. But it opened in 1904 as Interlake School, one of architect James Stephen's creations. For many years, Interlake School was the largest public elementary education institution in Seattle.

Guild 45th Theater

What's now the Guild 45th was opened in 1919 as the Paramount Theater (nine years before the debut of a much larger Paramount downtown). Located on North 45th Street between Meridian and Bagley avenues, the Paramount was originally a live stage venue, boasting two pipe organs. But by the 1930s, the place had become a motion picture playhouse owned by Hugh W. Bruen, who renamed it—what else?—Bruen's 45th Street. (The image at right shows the theater in 1934, when Barbara Stanwyck's tear-jerking, World War I–era romantic flick *Ever in My Heart* was playing there.) Today, the Guild 45th and its sister cinema, the Guild 45th II (opened in 1983 and located just two doors away), are part of the Landmark Theaters chain, specializing in smaller, independent, and foreign films. Director-producer Francis Ford Coppola has periodically screened his movies for test audiences at the Guild 45th.

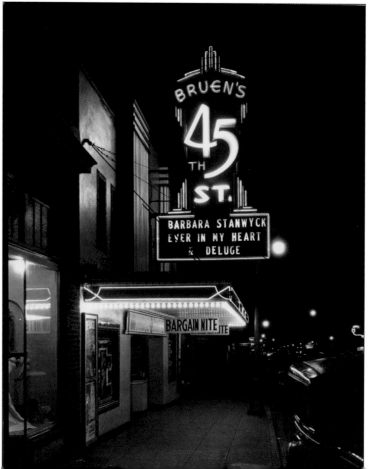

House of the Good Shepherd

This former residence for "wayward girls" is tucked somewhat off Wallingford's main drag, at North 50th Street and Sunnyside Avenue North. Opened in 1907, its construction was commissioned by the Sisters of the Good Shepherd, a cloistered Roman Catholic order devoted to the care and schooling of young women "of dissolute habits." It was designed by C. Alfred Breitung, a German immigrant who began practicing architecture in Seattle in 1900, and Vienna-born Theobold Buchinger, who'd worked on courthouses and breweries before joining Breitung in 1905. The Italianate, brick-and-stone House of the Good Shepherd was the first of several large Catholic institutions their partnership created. (Breitung and Buchinger also gave us Holy Names Academy on Capitol Hill.) The Sisters moved out of this structure in 1973; it was slated to be replaced by a shopping center, but neighborhood opposition killed that plan. The city of Seattle purchased the property in 1975, and the building (which long ago lost the cupola shown in the 1922 photo at left) is now a multipurpose community center and historic landmark.

Dick's Drive-in

There are still a couple of drive-in restaurants on Aurora Avenue, but the tradition of car-side cuisine in Seattle is mostly upheld these days by Dick's, a fast-food chain inaugurated in 1954 by Dick Spady and his business partners. The store on Northeast 45th Street in Wallingford is this enterprise's original outlet. On weekend days, space in the parking lot there is at a premium, and it's well worth taking in a little cholesterol just for the people-watching. This is a standard fueling stop for high-school and University of Washington students, but Dick's is also frequented by nostalgia-hungry adults.

The menu is pretty much restricted to burgers, pencil-thin French fries in grease-spotted bags, and shakes that defy easy sucking through a straw. There's no seating, so everybody has to dine behind the wheel or else drive to another location—just as they did half a century ago. There are four other Dick's locations: in Lower Queen Anne, Capitol Hill, Crown Hill, and Lake City.

UNIVERSITY DISTRICT

After the University of Washington relocated from downtown Seattle to its present home north of the city, a competition was held to determine who would design the first building on the new campus. The winner was Charles W. Saunders, who offered a four-story, turreted, French château-style edifice that must have stood out like a castle in the wilderness when it was completed in 1895. (The photo below shows it in about 1901.) Initially called the Administration Building, it was renamed Denny Hall in 1910 for Arthur A. Denny, who had helped found the university and gave it its original site. Years later, UW professor Edmond S. Meany recalled that the location of Denny Hall had been chosen during a tour of the then-undeveloped campus by university regents and other officials. "Regent [David] Kellogg stuck his umbrella into the ground where they decided the corner-stone should be," Meany explained. "Fortunately, architect Saunders took careful bearings of that fine location for it was the only logged-off land and some fellow stole the umbrella." The belfry atop this building contains the university's original 1861 bell.

"The Ave"

In 1890, just prior to the University of Washington moving into this area, developer James A. Moore went to work clearing lots and grading roads for a new town site he called Brooklyn. He envisioned it as primarily industrial. However, when the state legislature announced in early 1891 that the university would be relocated here, Moore was glad to spice his sales patter with that information. Only a few months later, the neighborhood got another boost when its few hundred residents voted to annex Brooklyn to the city of Seattle. The "U District," as it's now known ("Brooklyn" having long ago disappeared from maps except as the name of a street west of the UW campus), has prospered as a result of its proximity to Washington's leading public institution of higher education. Its main drag, University Way—or, more familiarly, "The Ave"—has become a lively commercial strip. The community boasts that it gave the city its first and only female mayor, Bertha K. Landes, in the late 1920s. A few remaining used bookstores and funky cafés, plus the annual U District Street Fair in May, keep a bit of this quarter's countercultural soul alive. *Above:* University Way looking north from 43rd Street, circa 1925.

Suzzallo Library

Original plans for the UW campus were prepared in 1891 by architects William Boone and William H. Willcox. But due to flaws in the legislation creating that institution, construction was halted soon after it began, and the Boone & Willcox plan was subsequently tossed. More than two decades later, designers Carl Gould and Charles H. Bebb developed another master plan. Gould also created for the campus one of its most beautiful buildings, the soaring "Collegiate Gothic" Suzzallo Library. Its construction was initiated by university president Henry Suzzallo after World War I. But rising costs for that and other UW projects provoked a showdown in the mid-1920s between the ambitious Suzzallo and Washington's new governor, the frugal Roland Hartley. Hartley finally won, forcing Suzzallo's dismissal in 1926. However, following Suzzallo's death in 1933—a year after Hartley was turned out of office by voters—the library he'd championed was named in his honor. *Above:* Suzzallo Library in 1926, the year it was completed. An addition on the south end in the mid-1930s greatly expanded the building.

Left: Many UW students find a home away from home in the cavernous Graduate Reading Room at Suzzallo library.

Student Housing

Efforts were made during the early 1900s to upgrade the university's curriculum, boost its faculty numbers, and find room for all the new classes being initiated and for all the young people being enrolled. In 1898, there were fewer than 200 students at the UW; by 1903, there were more than 700. That number jumped above 1,000 in 1905. Unfortunately, the construction of new facilities lagged far behind need. Students met in crowded classrooms, and though two dormitories had been built in the mid-1890s—Lewis Hall (for men) and Clark Hall (for women)—there wasn't always housing available. As a result of those inadequacies, the UW was ranked near the bottom in a survey of 46 U.S. universities. *Left:* Students were responsible for providing their own bedding and were free to decorate their rooms as they wished. Here we see a woman's dorm room, circa 1905.

Olympic Champion Crew Team

The University of Washington is more widely known for its football and basketball teams (both called the Huskies) than it is for its rowing squad. However, the crew team has proved itself more than able over the last century. Rowing seemed a natural sport for student athletes living and playing so close to the water. The university fielded its first men's rowing team in 1903, despite a lack of college competition on the Pacific Coast. By the end of that decade, the UW was the coast's dominant rowing team. And in 1936, the team gained international acclaim by winning the gold medal for rowing at that year's Olympic Games in Berlin, defeating strong squads from Italy and Germany. It's said that Adolf Hitler was particularly displeased with the UW's showing. Members of that championship team were (left to right, standing): Roger Morris, Charles Day, Gordon B. Adam, John G. White, James B. McMillin, George E. Hunt, Joseph Rantz, Don B. Hume, and (kneeling) Robert G. Moch.

Kent State Shooting Protests

On May 4, 1970, four students who'd been among a crowd protesting the American invasion of Cambodia were shot to death by National Guard troops at Kent State University in Ohio. Fearing more violence, 37 university presidents—including Charles Odegaard from the UW—sent telegrams to President Richard Nixon, urging the removal of U.S. troops from Southeast Asia. On May 5, more than 7,000 UW students and faculty members demonstrated by marching from campus onto nearby Interstate 5, bound for a rally at the Federal Courthouse downtown *(left)*. They shut down traffic as they went but encountered minimal resistance from state troopers. The students eventually exited the freeway and continued to their rally. After a brief bout of police-on-protestor violence two days later, Mayor Wes Uhlman decided to close I-5 on May 8 and allow 15,000 antiwar activists to march from the university to another rally downtown.

Blue Moon Tavern

You wouldn't know it to look at this small joint near the corner of Eighth Avenue Northeast and Northeast 45th Street, but the Blue Moon Tavern is a cultural landmark. It serves as a link to Seattle's hippie, beatnik, and literary heritage. Opened in 1934 in what had previously been a garage, the Blue Moon first became popular with UW students, who chafed under a ban on alcohol sales within one mile of the campus; the Blue Moon was located just beyond that limit. (The alcohol ban wasn't lifted until 1967.) During the 1950s, this tavern gained a reputation as the hangout for authors and poets, among them Theodore Roethke, Carolyn Kizer, Richard Hugo, and—when he was in town— Allen Ginsberg. UW professors maligned by the Canwell Committee once found a retreat here, and it's said that novelist Tom Robbins tried to place a collect phone call to Pablo Picasso from the Blue Moon, but Picasso refused the call. Refurbished in the 1980s, this watering hole was threatened a decade later with demolition. However, an energetic campaign ultimately saved the Blue Moon for the next generation of thinkers and drinkers.

FROM TRAINS TO TEN-SPEEDS

IN 1885, LAWYER Daniel Hunt Gilman and Judge Thomas Burke incorporated the Seattle, Lake Shore & Eastern Railroad. Within two years, the rails extended north from the Seattle waterfront to Salmon Bay, crossed over to Ballard, and then headed east along the northwest shore of Lake Washington. By 1888, the line ran as far as Fall City to the east and Snohomish County to the north. The Northern Pacific Railway assumed control of this route in the 1890s, and a merger in 1970 placed it under the auspices of the Burlington Northern Railroad. But BN quickly abandoned the rail bed, and plans were made to turn it into a public biking and walking path. In August 1978, the first 12.1-mile segment of the Burke-Gilman Trail was dedicated, connecting Gas

Works Park in Wallingford with the town of Kenmore, at the north end of Lake Washington. The trail has since been extended west to Ballard and reaches Issaquah in the east by way of the Sammamish River Trail and East Lake Sammamish Trail. All told, this mostly flat route is now almost 40 miles long and is especially popular with fair-weather bicyclists and Rollerbladers. *Above:* A Seattle, Lake Shore & Eastern train makes a stop in the woods, circa 1887.

Frosh Pond

This water feature in the southeast corner of the UW campus got its present name from an early 20th-century tradition, whereby sophomore students gave freshmen honorary dunkings here. The graceful, multijet fountain at the center of Frosh Pond is named after a university regent, Joseph Drumheller, who gave it to the UW in 1961 to help celebrate the centennial of that institution's founding. The buildings on the left and right are Johnson Hall and Mary Gates Hall, respectively. In the distance on the right is Suzzallo Library. During the 1909 Alaska-Yukon-Pacific Exposition, this pond was known as Geyser Basin, and it was the fair's central focal point.

ALASKA-YUKON-PACIFIC EXPOSITION

On June 1, 1909, President William Howard Taft, seated in the East Room of the White House, depressed a telegraph key shaped from Klondike gold and thus triggered a gong at the University of Washington campus, opening Seattle's Alaska-Yukon-Pacific Exposition (A-Y-P). By day's end, almost 80,000 adults and children had passed through the entrance gates of this city's first world's fair. They came to rub elbows with dignitaries, such as Democratic presidential candidate William Jennings Bryan, New York Governor Charles Evans Hughes, and Taft himself, who was stung painfully by a bee during his stopover. They came to wander through dozens of state and international pavilions, with their exhibits of foodstuffs, handicrafts, industrial goods, and sometimes curious artwork (including a giant elephant, made from English walnuts, in the California Building). They came to stroll among the expo's elegant edifices and fountains and well-manicured grounds, the last of those designed by the Olmsted brothers. And they came to enjoy the thrill rides, games of chance, and exotic entertainments of the Pay Streak, this fair's midway. By the time the A-Y-P closed on October 16, it had welcomed more than 3.7 million visitors. *Below:* The Court of Honor, with the domed U.S. Government Building in the distance, and the Arctic Circle and Geyser Basin (today's Frosh Pond) in the foreground.

Inset: A 1909 postcard advertising the fair's amusement park component, the Pay Streak

Forestry Building

A seeming exception to the classical styling of so many A-Y-P edifices was the monumental Forestry Building, located on Nome Circle, on the fairgrounds' east side. Constructed of raw, old-growth logs and unfinished timber, it was modeled on a somewhat smaller wooden temple that was featured at the 1905 World's Fair in Portland, Oregon. Seattle's version was designed by Charles W. Saunders and George W. Lawton, and despite its rough character, it echoed the fair's classical forms. This was especially true of its sweeping, 320-foot entrance facade (*above*), across which stretched a succession of 50,000-pound log columns supporting a balcony and a roof with twin cupolas. After the fair, the Forestry Building was used by the university for a variety of educational purposes. It was demolished in 1931 after being undermined by beetles.

Pay Streak

As was common with world's fairs during the 19th and 20th centuries, the A-Y-P's earnest, educational exhibits and grand architecture were balanced out with an amusement center full of mirth-inducing delights. In the case of Seattle's first exposition, this entertainment midway was called the Pay Streak and stretched along the site's western border. Among the draws were a Chinese Village and Ferris wheel (*above*), the Vacuum Tube Railway, the pyramidal Temple of Palmistry, the Upside-Down House, Alkali Ike's Wild West & Indian Show, a Streets of Cairo attraction, the Haunted Swing, and L. A. Thompson's Scenic Railway (a roller coaster weaving through mountain environments).

Transcontinental Auto Race

In 1909, automobiles were still new enough in Seattle that most residents had never ridden in one. Yet this fair celebrated their potential with a transcontinental car race that began in New York City on June 1, 1909. The event was sponsored by M. Robert Guggenheim, heir to his family's mining fortune, and promoted the "good roads" movement. It's said that almost three dozen competitors had planned to take part, but only six vehicles showed up at the starting line: an Italian-made Itala and five U.S.-manufactured cars—a Shawmut, an Acme, a Stearns, and two Model T Fords. Twenty-three days later, after weathering rain, mud, and the Cascade Mountains' near-impenetrable Snoqualmie Pass, the first two vehicles reached Seattle. Coming in first was one of the Model Ts, but it was later disqualified because its drivers had replaced their engine en route. As a result, Guggenheim's $3,500 in prize money went to the second-place finisher, the larger Shawmut. *Below:* The first-place-finishing Ford, with Guggenheim grinning behind the steering column to the left of the driver, and Henry Ford himself standing to the right of the driver.

While the Pay Streak specialized in frivolities, even it had a thing or two to teach fairgoers. Along its crowded length could be found huge, artistic re-creations of historical turning points, such as the Civil War Battle of Gettysburg and, in a structure of particularly martial character *(left)*, the 1862 Battle of Hampton Roads, also called the Battle of the *Monitor* and the *Merrimack*, which pitted two ironclad vessels against each other in the waters off Sewell's Point, Virginia. (That clash ended inconclusively, with both the Union and Confederacy claiming victory.) In addition, there were "ethnographic attractions" professing to show how "primitive peoples" lived. The most popular of those were a pseudo-Eskimo village (complete with dogsleds, despite the fact that it was summer in Seattle) and a tiny collection of grass-roofed huts inhabited by Igorrote (or Igorot) natives of the Philippines, who demonstrated their traditional crafts and shocked constitutionally delicate observers by dancing in their loincloths. *Above:* Local Masonic Lodge members try to go native with the spear-wielding Igorrotes.

RAVENNA

What's now the Ravenna neighborhood north of the University District was blanketed with Douglas firs when William Bell (of Belltown renown) first purchased property there in the late 1800s. The area's other noteworthy feature was a meandering creek that carried seasonal overflow from Green Lake out through a deep primordial ravine and into Lake Washington's Union Bay. Since that gorge was near-impossible to build in, it was left as wild parkland. In 1888, William W. Beck, a Presbyterian minister from Kentucky, and his wife, Louise, purchased 400 acres in the area. They quickly began clearing their land for home sales but decided there was still more profit to be made from their share of the ravine. So they fenced off 60 acres of it and called it Ravenna Natural Park. Seattleites were happy to travel out there on the weekends to enjoy the trails and picnic grounds the Becks had created. Also worth seeing were the larger trees in the park—15 to 20 feet in diameter and 300 feet tall—which the Becks had named after such famous figures as Robert E. Lee and Theodore Roosevelt. Unfortunately, most of those estimable evergreens were felled after the city of Seattle acquired Ravenna Park through eminent domain in 1911. *Below: A pair of children ford Ravenna Creek, circa 1891.*

A Rare Natural Sanctuary

Not only did this park's old-growth timber stands disappear during the early 20th century, but so did most of Ravenna Creek. The lowering of Green Lake in 1911 and of Lake Washington five years later eliminated that stream's flow and purpose. Part of its former bed now lies buried beneath Ravenna Boulevard, while only a short segment—twisting through Ravenna Park and its more compact neighbor to the west, Cowen Park (donated to the city in 1907)—continues to flow, fed by small springs and a wetland in the northwest corner of Cowen Park. Despite all these changes, Ravenna Park (left) remains a rare and popular piece of wilderness within the city limits, its wide trails frequented by strolling families and sweating runners.

"Support the Berkeley Struggle"

Ravenna Park has a reputation for peacefulness, but that was upset in the early summer of 1969, after the two-month-old Helix—Seattle's first "underground newspaper"—called for people to gather there in protest on Sunday, June 1. The cause of complaint was California Governor Ronald Reagan's recent decision to clear UC Berkeley students from "People's Park," a new commons they were planting for themselves on a derelict site. Reagan's orders had led to violence, and the Helix wanted Seattle's young people to turn out at Ravenna Park in solidarity. The event was successful, but it precipitated more than a few complaints from neighbors about "drum-beating, recorder-playing, stick-tapping hippies." Oh, and they didn't like the pot smoke either.

Washington Children's Home

Ravenna was once recognized for its social welfare agencies. Around 1914, the Volunteers of America acquired an old brick mansion on 35th Avenue Northeast and turned it into the Theodora, a group residence for single women and their offspring. Only a few blocks west of there, at Northeast 65th Street and 32nd Avenue Northeast, was the receiving facility of the nonprofit Washington Children's Home Society. Founded in the mid-1890s by the Reverend Harrison D. Brown and his wife, Libbie Beach Brown, that organization sought to place abandoned children with foster families rather than in orphanages—a new idea at the time. It operated out of the Green Lake area until a 1907 fire destroyed its building and claimed the lives of two infants. The society's move to Ravenna in 1908 gave it a grander, pillared home and enhanced presence. Now known as the Children's Home Society of Washington, it operates statewide. *Right:* Residents of the home pose with their favorite dolls, circa 1921.

West Seattle/South Seattle/Mount Baker

THE OTHER SEATTLE

Most people visualize Seattle as occupying the land from North 145th Street—the northern city limits—down to South Holgate Street, just below Safeco Field, where the Seattle Mariners baseball team plays. For some reason, neighborhoods farther south receive comparatively scant attention, except as places to drive *through* on the way to Seattle-Tacoma International Airport (Sea-Tac) or the Stan Sayres Memorial Hydroplane Pits, where the Chevrolet Cup races are held every summer as part of Seattle's Seafair celebration. Even West Seattle, the cradle of this town's birth, doesn't attract as much notice as the suburbs on the east side of Lake Washington. But it's not as if Seattle's southernmost quarters haven't earned their way into the history books.

During the Great Depression of the 1930s, after tens of thousands of people lost their jobs in Seattle and surrounding King County—only to then lose their homes as well—a nine-acre "Hooverville" sprang up around the foot of South Atlantic Street, near where Safeco Field now stands. This was an encampment of the dispossessed and destitute, comprising some 600 men and women who raised shabby, unheated shacks made of scrap lumber, broken chunks of cement, and other materials picked up along the waterfront. They dubbed their shantytown "Hooverville" in a backhanded tribute to President Herbert Hoover, who many believed had been ineffective in stopping America's economic decline.

Seattle's Hooverville was established in 1931 and lasted through most of that decade.

SEX AND SUDS
It was south of downtown, too, where the world's first gas station is said to have opened and where the county "poor farm" was once located, on the banks of the Duwamish River. It was also there that one of the largest houses of prostitution ever conceived was constructed during the early part of the 20th century—a contribution to this city's ribald past made, in large part, by the first of only two Seattle mayors ever to be recalled from office by the voters, Hiram C. Gill.

Above: Kubota Gardens in South Seattle pays tribute to Seattle's Japanese heritage.

Left: "Hooverville," circa 1937

Baseball found its initial following in South Seattle and was played for half a century in a pair of wooden ballparks located at the same intersection. But it wasn't the Mariners doing the swinging and base-running back then—it was the Rainiers. The team belonged to a brewery owner, which explained why newspaper headline writers, always looking to shorten references and squeeze more information into their decks, frequently referred to the Rainiers as the "Suds."

BOEING'S IMPACT
The city's first automobile races were staged in South Seattle in the summer of 1905 on a one-mile-long, circular dirt track called The Meadows (above, circa 1909), which had been built for horse racing near Georgetown. It was also at The Meadows, seven years later, that Seattle's first airplane death occurred.

During a demonstration flight, pilot J. Clifford Turpin lost altitude and crashed into the grandstand, killing one spectator and injuring another dozen. Apparently not believing in bad luck omens, the city paved over The Meadows in the late 1920s to create its first municipal airport, Boeing Field. That name, of course, honored William E. Boeing, who had constructed his original rickety planes at a facility on Lake Union before moving production to a mammoth shed on the Duwamish, not far from Boeing Field. But there was evidently an ulterior motive to that airport's dedication. The Boeing Airplane Company, which had won a major airmail-delivery contract in 1926, wanted a bigger landing strip from which to operate. Even then, the company was among the largest in King County, and local leaders didn't want it to move somewhere else, such as Los Angeles, which Bill Boeing had suggested as an alternative location. So the Port of Seattle found money for construction, and Boeing Field was dedicated on July 26, 1928. It served as the city's airline traffic hub until 1947, when Sea-Tac was opened to commercial service. (Airlines stopped flying into Boeing Field in the '50s.) Sea-Tac is now the 17th busiest airport in the United States.

SHIFTING CULTURES
South Seattle was once home to industrious Japanese and Italian farmers. In fact, so many Italians gathered at the northern reach of Rainier Valley that it came to be known as "Garlic Gulch." Sadly, the vast majority of Italian shops and restaurants disappeared long ago. There are Southeast Asian eateries scattered along these streets, but the Japanese heritage is most strongly felt at Kubota Gardens on Renton Avenue South. Established as a private nursery in the 1920s, the property was purchased by the city in 1987 and was turned into a public park. More evident in South Seattle is the impact of African Americans. During the 1970s, economic woes and Boeing's massive layoffs turned Rainier Valley into one of Seattle's poorest neighborhoods. Black families moved in and built churches and businesses. Today, this sector hosts the Northwest African American Museum (2300 South Massachusetts Street), housed in a 1909 school building and featuring displays about local black artists and the life of George Washington Bush, Washington's first African American resident in the 1840s.

And let's not forget West Seattle, where this city's story started. It's also where you will find Seattle's highest point (520 feet above sea level, at the intersection of 35th Avenue Southwest and Southwest Myrtle Street). And where one of the city's most popular beaches can be found, together with a historic lighthouse and an eight-foot-tall replica of the Statue of Liberty, which was originally a gift from the Boy Scouts of America in 1952 but was replaced by a recast replica in 2007. If Seattle didn't become the New York of the West, as promised, it at least has this consolation prize.

Right: Dedication of Boeing Field, 1928

WEST SEATTLE

On the afternoon of November 13, 1905, more than 1,000 people gathered at Alki Point in front of the old Stockade Hotel to witness the unveiling of this granite monument marking the site where the Denny Party landed in 1851. Participating were 3 of the 24 people who had stepped off the schooner *Exact* on that same date 54 years before: Carson Boren, Mary Low Sinclair, and Rolland H. Denny, the last of whom was just ten weeks old when the pioneers arrived at West Seattle. Together with descendents of three other 1851 settlers, they lifted a flag from this obelisk marking the "Birthplace of Seattle" and inscribed in recognition of Denny Party members. In 1926, a decade before the Stockade Hotel was torn down, the obelisk was moved across Alki Avenue to its present location at the foot of 63rd Avenue Southwest. On November 13, 1951, General Douglas MacArthur helped commemorate the 100th anniversary of the Denny Party's landing and presided over the burying of a time capsule near the pylon, one of two that are due to be opened in 2051. *Left:* Rolland H. Denny returns to study the monument in 1938. He died the next year at age 87.

Alki Point Light Station

It's said that there has been a beacon at Alki Point, warning ships to steer clear of this headland's treacherous shoals, ever since the mid-1870s, when farmer Hans Martin Hanson first hung a lantern off the shore of this southern entrance to Elliott Bay. In 1910, Congress finally appropriated money to construct a lighthouse on the wedge-shape tip of Alki. The Alki Point Light Station (left, circa 1925), with its 37-foot octagonal tower and Fresnel lens, was completed three years later. In 1918, its kerosene or acetylene lamp was replaced with an electric version. Since 1984, the lighthouse has been fully automated, eliminating the need for a lighthouse keeper. The exterior of this structure, which is listed on the Washington Heritage Register, still looks essentially as it did in 1913. It's one of eight lighthouses around Puget Sound that is open to visitors.

Admiral Theater

There's been a movie theater operating near the northwest corner of California Avenue Southwest and Southwest Admiral Way ever since 1919—just not the same one. Originally, it was the Portola Theater, with a handsome Wicks organ and a busy schedule of newsreels, comedy shorts, and feature films—many of which the management promised would be "first runs in the state." In 1942, though, the Portola was expanded and reopened as the 1,000-seat Admiral Theater. Named by way of a contest open to all West Seattle residents, the Admiral was designed by B. Marcus Priteca, who capitalized on the winning moniker by giving this showplace a nautical Moderne style, complete with portholes and waves decorating the facade and seahorses riding exit signs. In 1973, the Admiral was divided into two 430-seat theaters; it closed altogether in 1989. Fortunately, a neighborhood preservation campaign, declaring "Don't Sink the Admiral," won the movie house landmark status and found new owners committed to its survival. *Left:* Today, the Admiral is a popular second-run theater. *Right:* Opening night at the Admiral, January 22, 1942, showing *Week-end in Havana*, with John Payne, Alice Faye, and Carmen Miranda.

Alki Beach

Puget Sound isn't typically considered a good place to go swimming, mostly because its waters don't get much warmer than 56 degrees Fahrenheit. However, the establishment of a streetcar connection from downtown Seattle to Alki Beach in 1907—the same year that West Seattle was incorporated into the city—brought tens of thousands of people out looking for relief on hot summer days. By 1911, the city had purchased much of the shoreline along what's now Alki Avenue and had erected a bathing and recreation pavilion. (That wooden structure appears in the center of the photo at right, taken in 1916.) During the early 20th century, families traveled out to Alki to swim, stroll the seawall and boardwalk that stretched southwest along the Sound, and attend concerts at a covered, octagonal bandstand hanging out over the water. Nowadays, Seattleites have air-conditioning to keep them cool, and Alki Beach—the rather rocky 2.5-mile-long strip between Alki Point and Duwamish Head—is sparsely occupied, even on scorching days, with picnickers, volleyball players, and young women in bathing suits skimpy enough to have caused the early Alki beachgoers to turn red—and not necessarily from the sun.

Left: This present-day photo of Alki Beach shows Seattle's eight-foot replica of the Statue of Liberty.

Luna Park

Charles I. D. Looff knew how to move fast when he saw an opportunity. The one-time furniture carver, who had created the first carousel for New York's Coney Island, visited Alki Beach in early 1907. In June, he opened Luna Park at Duwamish Head, the beach's northernmost point. An ambitious, dozen-acre "seaside pleasure resort" erected on pilings over the water, Luna Park featured a "Great Figure-Eight" roller coaster, a "Giant Whirl" circle swing, an aquarium, a skating rink, a dance pavilion, a "Shoot-the-Chutes" ride, and—in a nod to Looff's artistic roots—a carousel with prancing horses and "sneaky tigers" housed in a round, onion-domed edifice (seen at the top right in this photograph). For seven summers, Looff's amusement park drew entertainment-starved locals to the West Seattle shore. But a scandal involving underage girls mixing with overintoxicated men at the facility's "longest bar on the bay" soured Luna Park's reputation. Most of its attractions closed in 1913, though its saltwater natatorium managed to remain in business until a fire burned it, along with what remained of the park, in 1931.

ROLL 'EM!

MANY A MOVIE-WATCHER is familiar with Seattle, thanks to the 1993 romantic film *Sleepless in Seattle*, starring Meg Ryan and Tom Hanks. Even though the city is rather distorted in that picture (a quick boat ride from Lake Union to Alki Beach? Hah!), it long served as Seattle's best publicity tool. However, this city has more extensive experience in front of the camera than that. *Tugboat Annie* (1933), starring Marie Dressler and Wallace Berry as quarreling husband and wife tugboat operators, may have been the earliest film shot here. The city has since provided a setting for *It Happened at the World's Fair* (1963), starring Elvis Presley and the Space Needle; *McQ* (1974), with John Wayne as a Dirty Harry-like cop living on a houseboat in Fremont; *The Parallax View* (1974), a political thriller with Warren Beatty; *An Officer and a Gentleman* (1982), starring Richard Gere as an aspiring fighter pilot; *Frances* (1982), the tragic tale of Seattle native and film star Frances Farmer (played by Jessica Lange); and *Life or Something Like It* (2002), another romantic comedy, this one starring Angelina Jolie and Edward Burns. In addition, the 1990s TV sitcom *Frasier* was filmed here, as were the 2000 TV remake of *The Fugitive* and the 1973 teleflick *The Night Strangler*, in which Darren McGavin played a modern-day reporter pursuing an "undead" murderer who'd been living under Pioneer Square since the mid-1800s.

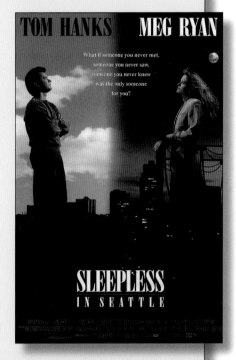

SOUTH SEATTLE

In 1912, the Union Pacific Railroad constructed this 12-story brick behemoth (below, circa 1918) on Utah Avenue, south of downtown and convenient to both rail and streetcar lines. It hoped to entice Chicago-based Sears, Roebuck and Company to occupy the building as the mail-order business's first Washington branch. That plan worked. Sears moved in and got busy right away, sending out everything from hats and cooking sets to girdles and farming equipment—pretty much anything its catalog custom-ers in the West wanted. Sears expanded over the decades and eventually opened retail space in this facility, serving as the initial place of employ-ment for many a local student. But after raising other outlets across the region, Sears put the 1.8-million-square-foot building up for sale in 1987. It's now the headquarters of Starbucks. To help commemorate its occu-pancy, Starbucks embellished the clock tower atop this building with the head of its mermaid icon *(inset)*.

"World's First Service Station"

Even before Henry Ford introduced the world's first affordable automobile, the mass-produced Model T, in 1908, Seattle is said to have opened the world's first gas station. In 1907, John McLean, the head of sales in Washington for Standard Oil (Chevron) of California, bought a chunk of land at the intersection of Western Avenue and Holgate Street on the Seattle waterfront, opposite Standard's main regional depot (and south of today's Safeco Field). With help from engineer Henry Harris, McLean put together a feed line from the main Standard storage tank to a 6-foot-tall, 30-gallon galvanized tank outfitted with a glass gauge and a convenient dispensing hose (shown in the bottom right corner of the photo at left, circa 1907). Prior to this innovation, what few drivers there were in Seattle purchased gasoline in refillable, five-gallon cans from livery stables or general stores. A plaque commemorating the "world's first service station" can now be found at Seattle's Waterfront Park.

Hiram Gill's Bordello

Of all the men (and one woman) who have served as mayor of Seattle, none was more corrupt than Hiram C. Gill. A former city council president, Gill was elected mayor in 1910 and right away started turning Seattle into a wide-open town. *McClure's* magazine reported that "thirty or forty gambling-places opened up" under his administration. His hand-picked police chief, Charles W. Wappenstein *(inset)*, a one-time Pinkerton man and former midwestern cop, was found to have taken bribes to protect illegal gambling establishments and houses of prostitution and was sent to the state penitentiary. And Gill hadn't been warming the mayor's seat for long before he authorized the construction of a 500-room brothel on Beacon Hill (shown at right, circa 1910). Seattleites finally had enough of Gill's antics and recalled him from office in 1911; amazingly, he was reelected in 1914 on a promise to end the very vice he'd encouraged before. Meanwhile, his Beacon Hill bordello was soon converted into a housing complex called the Lester Apartments. It stood until 1951, when a B-50 "Superfortress" bomber with engine trouble crashed into the building, destroying it and killing 11 people.

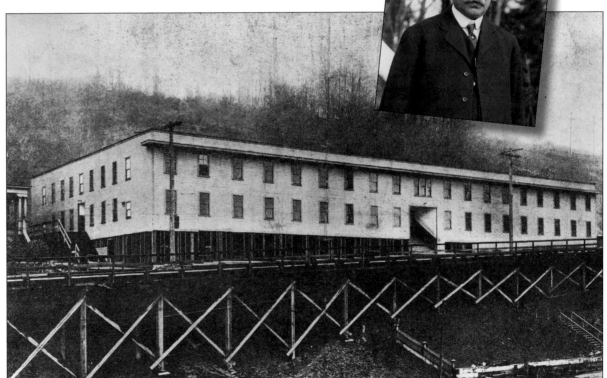

Georgetown City Hall

Of all the once-independent hamlets that were eventually incorporated into Seattle, Georgetown—located south of downtown and west of Rainier Valley—is the only one whose city hall remains standing. During the late 19th century, the area became notorious for its race track, county poor farm, and proliferation of breweries. In 1890, Julius Horton, the son of prominent Seattle banker Dexter Horton, platted the town site and named it after his own son, George. Interurban trains made it easily accessible to Seattle and encouraged capital development, as well as enhanced settlement of the area (many newcomers were German immigrants). Georgetown was finally incorporated in 1904, and five years later, it raised public funds to construct a brick city hall—with clock tower—at the intersection of 13th Avenue South and South Bailey Street. In addition to housing the local police and fire departments, jail, and mayor's office, that city hall was also Georgetown's first building with hot and cold running water. After resisting pressure for years, Georgetown finally annexed itself to Seattle in 1910. Its city hall is now listed on the National Register of Historic Places. However, the clock tower—once endangered by low-flying aircraft from Boeing Field—has been shortened. The photo at left shows the building with its original spire.

Seattle Brewing and Malting Company

In 1884, former San Francisco beer maker Edward F. Sweeney joined with a partner to create a small brewery in what would become Georgetown. Sweeney soon bought out his partner, and in 1889 he joined with the plant's brewmaster, Hans J. Claussen, to create the larger Claussen-Sweeney Brewing Company. In 1893, that enterprise merged with two other South Seattle breweries—most significantly the Bay View Brewing Company (shown at left in 1886), run by Andrew Hemrich—to form the Seattle Brewing and Malting Company, which became the world's sixth largest brewery and was best recognized for its Rainier-brand beer. Outside of a period between 1916 (when alcoholic beverages were outlawed in Washington) and the end of Prohibition in the 1930s, Rainier Beer was synonymous with Seattle. Emil Sick, who with his father acquired the old brewery in 1935, made sure of this by purchasing the Seattle Indians baseball team and renaming it the Rainiers. He also installed a giant neon "R" sign atop the original Claussen-Sweeney plant near South Spokane Street and Airport Way South. Rainier passed out of local hands in the late 1970s, and its landmark brewery—rising next to Interstate 5 in Georgetown—was closed in 1999. It now serves as the headquarters for the Tully's Coffee chain.

Boeing's Red Barn at Seattle's Museum of Flight

In 1916, budding aircraft entrepreneurs William E. Boeing and G. Conrad Westervelt relocated their operations from Lake Union to a former shipyard building on the Duwamish River south of Seattle that they called the "Red Barn." A year later, they reincorporated their Pacific Aero-Products Company as the Boeing Airplane Company. Their two-story, gable-roofed Red Barn served as Boeing's "world headquarters" until the 1930s, when a larger facility was opened at Boeing Field (once Seattle's main passenger airport), on the Duwamish between Georgetown and Tukwila. In 1970, the Red Barn was sold to the Port of Seattle, and five years later it was moved to the south end of Boeing Field. The building was restored and reopened in 1983 as the first part of Seattle's Museum of Flight. Architect Ibsen Nelson's glass-and-steel Great Gallery, which showcases biplanes, military jets, early mail planes, and other aircraft, was built next door in 1987. Both structures are seen in the photograph below.

Hat n' Boots Gas Station

One of Seattle's more distinctive examples of roadside kitsch, the Hat n' Boots Texaco Gas Station *(above)* was built in 1955 at the corner of Corson Avenue South and East Marginal Way near Georgetown. Designed by Albert Poe and Lewis H. Nasmyth, it was supposed to be part of a "Frontier Village"-themed shopping center, but the rest of the complex went unconstructed for lack of funds. The giant cowboy hat atop the station office measured about 40 feet across; the 22-foot-tall male and female boots each contained a restroom; and the facility claimed nine convenient gas pumps. But the construction of Interstate 5 in the 1960s severely reduced traffic flows on other north–south routes, including Marginal Way, and cut revenues for businesses such as the Hat n' Boots. The station closed in 1988 and was left to deteriorate. Fortunately, preservationists began campaigning in the 1990s to save the Hat n' Boots. In late 2003, the landmark was moved to Georgetown's new Oxbow Park at 6400 South Corson Avenue, and restoration efforts began.

PLAY BALL!

Amateur baseball games were played in Seattle as far back as the 1870s, but it wasn't until 1890 that the first professional game was staged here, at Madison Park. Players from Seattle challenged others from Spokane, and the former squad won. In 1898, Daniel E. Dugdale, a former big-league catcher, came to Seattle on his way to join the Klondike Gold Rush but decided to stay in this city instead. He went on to speculate in real estate, worked as a cable-car grip man, and established a new Seattle baseball team, the Klondikers. Later, the portly Dugdale created and managed other upstart ball clubs of inconsistent success. However, he's best remembered

for the 1913 construction of Dugdale Park, the West Coast's first double-decked stadium, at Rainier Avenue South and South McClellan Street. In addition to regular Pacific Coast League games, that great wooden ballpark also hosted exhibition contests. One of those, in 1924, found New York Yankees pitcher George Herman "Babe" Ruth, nicknamed "The Sultan of Swat" for his batting prowess, joining local ballplayers in an all-star game promoted by the *Seattle Post-Intelligencer*. In nine times at bat, Ruth smacked three home runs. *Below:* Ruth at Dugdale Park, circa 1930.

Sick's Stadium

Dugdale Park remained a fixture on the West Coast baseball circuit until the summer of 1932, when a serial arsonist reduced it to ashes and smoke. After that, the Seattle team—then called the Indians—resorted to playing on the rocky grounds of Civic Field, known today as Memorial Stadium at Seattle Center. However, big changes were in the works. In the mid-1930s, after America's 13-year experiment with Prohibition was finally repealed and alcohol could be sold again, Tacoma-born brewer Emil Sick—who had spent the "dry years" making beer in Canada with his father—moved to Seattle and bought the Rainier Brewery. In late 1937, he also purchased the Indians, renamed the franchise the Rainiers, and started building a new concrete-and-steel stadium on the old Dugdale Park site. Some 12,000 fans showed up at Sick's Seattle Stadium (right, circa 1969) for the inaugural game in June 1938.

The minor-league Rainiers played at Sick's Stadium (later *Sicks'* Stadium) for 26 years. Seattleites loved that park. It boasted a covered grandstand (great for the city's unpredictable weather) and seating for 15,000—not including the spectators who preferred to watch for free from "Tightwad Hill," a knoll just beyond the left-field fence. Fans followed Rainiers players such as extra-thin third-baseman Dick "The Needle" Gyselman (shown in the photo at left, running toward first base in 1941), shortstop Bill Stump (who was apparently prone to forgetting the number of outs), and infielder Bill Schuster (called "Schuster the Rooster," because he would clamber up the grandstand screen and crow like a barnyard bird). In 1946, the Seattle Steelheads—part of the West Coast Baseball Association's Negro League—began playing at Sick's Stadium while the Rainiers were on the road. Unfortunately, increased TV coverage of baseball games in the 1950s caused attendance to drop, and Emil Sick sold his team to the major-league Boston Red Sox in 1961. The Sox subsequently sold the franchise to the California Angels, which renamed it the Seattle Angels.

Safeco Field

It wasn't until 1969 that Seattle won its own major league baseball team, the Pilots. While a new domed sports stadium, the Kingdome, was being built immediately south of Pioneer Square, the Pilots made do playing at an insufficiently expanded Sicks' Stadium. By the time the Kingdome finally opened in 1977, the Pilots had already left town for Milwaukee, Wisconsin; Sicks' Stadium was torn down in 1979. Also in 1977, the city welcomed a new major league franchise, the American League's Seattle Mariners. The team played for most of the next two decades in the closed, sterile, and much-despised Kingdome, which was demolished with explosives in 2000. Since 1999, the Mariners have made their home in the retractable-roofed Safeco Field *(below)*, a classic-looking ballpark just south of the former Kingdome site. A second stadium, Qwest Field, home of the National Football League's Seattle Seahawks, was opened on the former Kingdome site in 2002.

SOUTHEAST LAKE SHORE

Until at least the late 1890s, the forested ridge separating the Rainier Valley from Lake Washington was better known for sawmills than residences. But in 1905, property developer J. C. Hunter began platting substantial acreage on that ridgeline, land that had once belonged to pioneer David Denny. His intention was to create a picturesque, upper-income residential district. He called the subdivision "Mount Baker," presumably because it offered remarkable views of 10,778-foot Mount Baker, part of the Cascade Range in Whatcom County, north of Seattle. While not the city's first planned community, Mount Baker was among the first to be integrated with the system of parks that the Olmsted brothers mapped out in 1903. With help from both that Massachusetts landscaping firm and Edward O. Schwagerl, who had served as Seattle's parks superintendent during the 1890s, Mount Baker became a showplace of grand homes, a very active community club, and a beautified natural buffer. Its most prominent landscaping venture was the Olmsted-designed Colman Park, 24.3 acres of trees and boulevards leading down to Lake Washington. There's also Mount Baker Park, essentially a ravine boulevard connecting to Colman Park (shown below in the early 20th century).

Nº 107. BOULEVARD IN MT. BAKER PARK, SEATTLE, WASHINGTON.

The Rumrunner's Residence

This mini-mansion at 3757 South Ridgeway Place (left, circa 1925) once belonged to the notorious Roy Olmstead. Quick and competent, he joined the Seattle Police Department in 1906 and rose through the ranks like a meteor. By 1917 he was a lieutenant—the youngest one on the force, with a "brilliant career" ahead of him. During that same era, though, Washington joined 22 other states in forbidding the manufacture and sale of alcohol. Booze was suddenly in short supply yet still in high demand. Olmstead knew the risks of smuggling liquor in from Canada, but he also knew the profits to be made. It didn't take a whole lot more convincing for this cop to turn criminal. By 1920, he had become the most audacious and successful rumrunner to work Seattle during Prohibition. However, Olmstead's second career ended abruptly in 1924, when police stormed his Mount Baker home, arrested him and his wife, and seized his business records. Fourteen months later, he was found guilty of violating the Prohibition Act. He was sentenced to four years at the McNeil Island Federal Penitentiary in south Puget Sound. He served his full term, but in 1935, President Franklin D. Roosevelt granted Olmstead a full pardon.

Seward Park

In contrast to some of the Olmsted brothers's more manicured preserves, Seward Park—occupying what had previously been known as the Bailey Peninsula, south of the Mount Baker neighborhood—was intended as a "wild" park. Thanks, apparently, to an abundance of poison oak, the old-growth timber stands there survived the rapacious attentions of early loggers. In 1892, Edward O. Schwagerl proposed that the city take over the peninsula as parkland, but critics thought it was too far from downtown to be worth buying. Fortunately, the Olmsteds agreed with Schwagerl, and in 1911, Seattle purchased the peninsula for $322,000 and named it after William H. Seward, the secretary of state who had negotiated America's acquisition of Alaska in 1867. The park is laced with trails and is popular with both bikers and picnickers. Wildlife, including wild rabbits, feral parrots, and bald eagles, is abundant there. *Right:* Keeping up a sporting tradition, two lumbermen compete in a log-rolling contest at Seward Park in 1938.

Mercer Island/Bellevue/Kirkland

EASTSIDE STORY

For decades now, Seattle has had a love-hate relationship with its neighboring communities on the east side of Lake Washington. "Boomburbs" such as Bellevue, Kirkland, Issaquah, and Redmond are alternately celebrated as the home of "world-class" companies, such as Microsoft and Costco, and derided as socially superficial, culturally bereft, and politically right-wing.

Seattleites could barely suppress their amusement when, in 2003, the Bellevue Art Museum—which had opened only two years before in an avant-garde building designed by architect Steven Holl—was forced to close. The reason for that shuttering? Not enough locals wanted to see its exhibits of contemporary conceptual art. When the facility reopened 20 months later, it was as the Bellevue *Arts* Museum. The slight name change reflected a shift away from challenging and esoteric works toward an emphasis on crafts, furniture design, and Northwest artists. That move was perhaps economically essential, but it also reaffirmed the negative opinions many Seattleites share of Eastside communities—that they have far more money than taste and even less history to claim.

On that last point, it's true that the Eastside is largely a 20th- and 21st-century phenomenon. While Kirkland can claim a few downtown structures dating from the 1890s, the term "Old

Bellevue" hardly finds justification in the modest, refurbished lineup of post–World War II stores and galleries bordering Bellevue's Main Street between 100th and Bellevue Way. And yes, there are examples of early 20th-century mansions east of Lake Washington that have become the centerpieces of parks or residential developments. But most of the structures there look as if they weren't even conceived until after Jimmy Carter left the White House.

Still, the Eastside's past is far more interesting than most Seattleites realize.

LOOKING BACK
During the 1880s, plans called for turning Kirkland into an industrial center able to compete with anything the American East Coast had to offer. At about the same time, the nucleus of an ambitious community, "East Seattle," took root on the west side of Mercer Island. Dreams of an electric railway encircling that isle, grand arboretums

Above: Women and children wade in Bellevue's Meydenbauer Bay, circa 1912.

Left: The Bellevue Arts Museum

abloom with flowers and exotic plantings, and a magnificent hotel surrounded by high-end homes were spread throughout newspaper reports—but were ultimately sacrificed against the rocks of the nation's second-worst financial depression, which began in 1893. Not long after that, in 1908, an artists' colony was founded south of downtown Bellevue. A 50-acre tract was platted, and Craftsman-style bungalows—accessible via winding, curbless streets—began going up among the site's abundant evergreens. The idea of a hamlet filled with sculptors, painters, and other bohemian types had its appeal, but it was more bourgeois sorts who ultimately came to dominate—the folks who could actually afford to buy the homes there. That colony still exists as Beaux Arts Village, a peaceful residential enclave that seems not only miles but years away from the metropolitan concrete of Bellevue.

DITTY CITY

Speaking of big dreamers, let us not forget James Ditty. A real-estate mogul who arrived on the Eastside in 1910, Ditty soon became convinced that Bellevue, which by the mid-1920s claimed only about 1,000 residents, was destined to be a big deal. So he started purchasing pastureland and strawberry fields and subsequently produced a model-city concept for the Eastside that featured bustling railroad yards, smoke-belching industrial plants, and (more than three decades before the Space Needle opened) an observation tower poking up from the middle of Mercer Island. To accelerate trade and passenger travel across Lake

Washington, he recommended replacing existing ferries with a trio of bridges and—believe it or not—a mass-transit system of dirigibles. Seattle cartoonists poked fun at "Ditty City," but the developer was eventually proved prescient. His property lay smack-dab in the middle of what would become Bellevue's expansion zone. By the 1940s, land that had cost Ditty a mere 1.5 cents per square foot was suddenly worth $3 a square foot, and he began selling off parcels, including ten acres that are part of today's Bellevue Square.

PUTTING ISSAQUAH ON THE MAP

And of course, it was in then tiny Issaquah, southeast of Bellevue, where the largest Ku Klux Klan rally ever held in Washington took place. In the 1920s, years after it had made its first black mark on post–Civil War America, a reborn Klan styled itself as a hyper-patriotic body essential to maintaining American values. It gained a substantial following among people who worried that the United States was becoming too liberal and too involved in international affairs. On July 26, 1924, the so-called Invisible Empire reportedly "put Issaquah on the map" with a gathering of tens of thousands of people who answered its invitation to "learn firsthand the exact nature of the work of the Klan." In a field west of Issaquah, a wooden cross was raised, 40 feet tall and 20 feet wide, lit by hundreds of electric bulbs. Families gathered to hear speeches about "Americanism" and watch some 250 northwesterners be "naturalized" as

Klan members. Yet a few years later, the KKK's influence and presence had all but vanished from the region. Today, the Issaquah cornfield where the Klansmen held their get-together is occupied by a shopping center.

Above: A Ku Klux Klan member captured by a Seattle photographer, circa 1923.

But that's not the only thing that has changed on the Eastside. In the 1960s, most of the morning commuter traffic was heading west from Bellevue and Kirkland, as people went to work in Seattle. Now, thanks to a concentration of high-tech enterprises on the Eastside, the stream is pretty heavy both ways. And the concentration of communities there is rivaling Seattle for population and political influence.

Like James Ditty, the Eastside may have the last laugh after all.

Right: Aerial view of the Evergreen Point Floating Bridge, circa 1967

FLOATING BRIDGES

From the 1870s through the 1940s, ferries carried passengers and vehicles across Lake Washington, the 22-mile-long inland basin that forms Seattle's eastern border. However, as communities on the lake's east side became both more populous and prosperous, ferries were hard-pressed to keep up with demand. In the 1920s, local engineer Homer M. Hadley, who had built concrete ships and barges, proposed constructing "a floating concrete highway, permanent and indestructible, across Lake Washington." *The Seattle Times* dismissed the notion as "unthinkable," especially given how rough the lake could become during heavy storms. Publisher Clarence B. Blethen wrote: "Imagine what would happen to automobiles trying to cross it! But worst of all, imagine what would happen if the thing came apart!" Nonetheless, with the backing of Washington State Highway director Lacey V. Murrow (the brother of famed broadcast journalist Edward R. Murrow), Hadley's two-way, four-lane bridge was built atop 25 hollow, anchored concrete pontoons and opened in June 1940. At the time of its dedication, the Lake Washington Floating Bridge (pictured in the postcard below) was the largest floating concrete structure in the world, stretching from Seattle's Mount Baker neighborhood across the north end of Mercer Island, and ending south of Bellevue. Known since 1967 as the Lacey V. Murrow Memorial Bridge, it now carries the Interstate 90 freeway.

Evergreen Point Floating Bridge

Seattleites got along rather well for most of a century without so much as *one* floating bridge hurtling the width of Lake Washington. Yet only two decades after the 3,387-foot-long Murrow Bridge opened, a *second* length of suspended concrete and steel was stretched between Seattle and the Eastside. That Evergreen Point Floating Bridge, located north of the previous span, is now the longest span of its kind in the world at 7,578 feet. It crosses the lake from the Montlake neighborhood and Lake Union on the west to Evergreen Point in Medina, west of Bellevue. Like its predecessor, this second roadway—which opened in August 1963—was originally a toll bridge, but transportation charges were lifted in 1979. The span carries State Route 520 across the lake. In 1988, it was renamed the Governor Albert D. Rosellini Bridge—Evergreen Point in honor of the Washington chief executive (1957–1965) who had vigorously pushed for its construction. *Right:* Keeping the Evergreen Point bridge afloat are 33 prestressed concrete pontoons, most measuring 360 feet long, 60 feet wide, and 14 feet, 9 inches deep. The pontoon shown here, under construction in May 1961, was built by the Guy F. Atkinson Construction Company at a West Seattle dry dock.

Life has been hard for Lake Washington's floating bridges. The Evergreen Point span is often closed during high winds, lest waves be carried up and over the traffic lanes. (Shown below is one particularly vigorous tempest beating at the bridge in 1970.) And it is currently stressed by having to carry more than 110,000 cars every day, when it was designed to transport only half that many. Meanwhile, part of the adjacent Murrow Bridge sank during a winter storm in 1990. Fortunately, it was closed for renovation at the time, with traffic having been shifted to a parallel span—the floating Homer M. Hadley Memorial Bridge—which had opened in June 1989.

MR. CALKINS'S CASTLE

IN 1887, ILLINOIS-BORN lawyer Charles Cicero "C. C." Calkins arrived in Seattle with more dreams than money. He quickly invested in real estate, including more than 160 acres on Mercer Island. His intention was to create a new town there, "East Seattle," anchored by an exquisite hotel. The press gushed over Calkins's plans. "East Seattle is not excelled as a place of residence in this section of the Pacific Northwest," proclaimed *Pacific Magazine* in 1890. Strict controls were placed on what could and could not be constructed in East Seattle, and landscaping was given priority throughout the town site. No less impressive was the Calkins Hotel (below, circa 1890), a three-story architectural amalgam of American railroad station and Swiss chalet designed by John Parkinson and his partner, Cecil Evers. Tourists came from far and wide to study that inn's detailing and marvel at its grand lobby staircase. Even President Benjamin Harrison, who swung through Seattle in May 1891, included in his itinerary a boat trip around Lake Washington and a stop at the spectacular Calkins Hotel. Sadly, the economic crash of 1893 took C. C. Calkins down with it. East Seattle failed to become the posh resort he had planned, and he sold the hotel. It was eventually turned into a private sanitarium before burning to its foundations in 1908.

Above: The Governor Albert D. Rosellini Bridge—Evergreen Point is often called the "520 bridge" by locals.

BELLEVUE

Seattle baker William Meydenbauer was one of the first homesteaders on the east side of Lake Washington in the 1860s, giving his name to the sheltered cove where he raised his cabin—near where modern downtown Bellevue now sits. Aaron Mercer, the brother of better-known pioneers Thomas and Asa Mercer, settled to the south of Meydenbauer Bay along what became Mercer Slough. The community that grew around them was reportedly named in the 1880s by Mathew S. Sharpe, its first postmaster, who had come from Bellevue, Indiana. He decided that his old hometown's moniker—which meant "beautiful view" in French—was just as fitting for this spot as any other. Not everyone was convinced. Thick forests and comparatively poor farmland on the east side of the lake discouraged many prospective settlers. But by the 1890s, after considerable logging had been done, Bellevue fruit and vegetable gardens proved their worth. Strawberry farming was particularly popular here. The photo below shows people picking berries in 1903 at what is today the intersection of Northeast Eighth and 104th streets. Beginning in 1925, Bellevue's annual Strawberry Festival became a highlight of summer life on the Eastside.

Bellevue Regional Library

While Seattle claims a bookish reputation, Bellevue does not. Slower to grow, the latter metropolis also took longer to construct a landmark library. The chaletlike version below was photographed in 1944. That building was replaced in the mid-1960s by an even less distinctive modernist box that only reinforced the notion—broadly retailed by Seattleites and others—that Bellevue was not an intellectual community. That attitude changed—at least somewhat—in 1993 when the three-story, 80,000-square-foot, high-tech Bellevue Regional Library opened on 110th Avenue Northeast, near Ashwood Park. Designed by Ev Ruffcorn of the Zimmer Gunsul Frasca Partnership, that red-sandstone-and-glass-faced facility *(bottom)* features an abundance of semiprivate reading and study spaces, a skylight-covered central atrium and wood-paneled ceilings, and plenty of well-padded chairs and small round tables, conducive to sitting and reading. Ruffcorn's edifice won a 1993 Award of Merit from the Seattle chapter of the American Institute of Architects, which is remarkable for a suburban library.

Whaling Boats

Bellevue is not usually associated with the rugged history of American whaling. Yet for seven months out of every year between 1919 and 1942, Meydenbauer Bay provided off-season berths for steel-hulled, steam-powered boats, their foredecks accessorized with deadly harpoon cannons. They were part of the American Pacific Whaling Company fleet, which hunted blue, sperm, and humpback whales in the frigid waters off the coast of Alaska. The opening of Seattle's ship canal in 1917 made it possible for such large vessels to anchor in Lake Washington, and the fresh water there conveniently killed the barnacles and teredo worms that clung to the ships' hulls. William Schupp, the head of American Pacific Whaling, moved his headquarters and home to Bellevue from Bay City, near Westport, on the Washington coast. His men spent their winters at docks on Meydenbauer Bay (shown above in 1925) caulking decks and sharpening harpoon blades, readying for their May departures to the Last Frontier. At one time, whaling was one of the largest industries in Bellevue, employing more than 200 people. However, World War II hostilities with Japan killed American Pacific Whaling's business. Its docks are now part of a waterfront park development.

Bellevue Square Mall

It wasn't the Northwest's first regional shopping center; that distinction belongs to Northgate Mall, which opened north of Seattle in 1950. However, Bellevue Square has certainly become a giant, vibrant magnet for consumers with extra cash to spend and hours to browse. Prior to World War II, the corner of Northeast Eighth Street and Bellevue Way Northeast was pretty quiet. The aerial photo displayed above, taken in about 1937, shows the intersection dominated by Lakeside Center on the right, a single-story edifice that featured a pharmacy, a supermarket, and a ten-cent store. Surrounding it were a chicken farm and blueberry farm. In 1946, though, a local builder and banker named Kemper Freeman, Sr., began developing his own commercial complex, Bellevue Shopping Square, at the same crossroads. This ambitious project was initially anchored by a Frederick & Nelson department store. Today, under the ownership of his son, Kemper Freeman, Jr., the shorter-named Bellevue Square (shown in the present-day photo at right) ranks among the largest and most successful malls on the West Coast, containing 1.3 million square feet of space and offering almost 200 stores. It is linked via a sky bridge to Lincoln Square, a mixed-use center containing more retail space along with a hotel and residential tower.

Above: Bellevue Square today is a shopping complex as well as an alternative town center where people hold business meetings and walk for excercise.

KIRKLAND

White families began settling around modern-day Kirkland as early as the 1870s. By the late 1880s, industrialist Peter Kirk was finally kicking development there into high gear. He was a steel mill owner from England who had ventured to the Pacific Northwest in search of property on which to construct an extensive new iron- and steelworks. Although initially considering Tacoma for his headquarters, Kirk was convinced by *Seattle Post-Intelligencer* publisher Leigh S. J. Hunt that convenient and plentiful sources of coal, iron, and limestone could be had on the east side of Lake Washington. It was a giddy Hunt who announced in his paper that Kirk

was going to create at Moss Bay "the Pittsburgh of the West," a town inevitably christened "Kirkland." By 1891, streets and building lots were platted, hotels and office buildings were planned, and as the *P-I* enthused, "a large foundry, machine shop, blacksmith shop, and pattern shop are in course of erection, and a sawmill is in operation" (the ironworks is shown below, circa 1892). However, the Panic of 1893 drove a stake into Kirk's and Hunt's dreams. Investors in the project withdrew, the mill was never completed, and Kirkland failed to become another gray-skied steel town. Thank goodness.

Peter Kirk Building

After the failure of his Bessemer steelworks, Peter Kirk retired to the San Juan Islands, north of Seattle, where he died in 1916. However, his name lives on. One of the downtown Kirkland edifices left over from all the industrial hoopla is the two-story Peter Kirk Building at the corner of Market Street and Seventh Avenue *(left)*. Ground was broken for that Victorian edifice in 1889. The building was constructed over the next two years of brick fired at a brick works in what's now Peter Kirk Park at Central Way and Third Street. The Kirkland Land & Improvement Company, which included an office for Kirk, originally occupied the second floor above a large mercantile and drugstore. Refurbished by the Creative Arts League, the building now houses the Kirkland Arts Center (below, present day). It has been listed in the National Historic Register since 1973.

Lake Street

The population of Kirkland now exceeds 45,000. But in 1925, when the photograph at right was taken, the city claimed only 2,000 residents. In this picture, Lake Street looks like a small-town thoroughfare plucked straight out of *The Andy Griffith Show*. Among the businesses lining the street's east side back then were a shoe-repair shop, real-estate offices, a hotel, a drugstore, and clothing shops. On the hill in the distance is Central School.

Left: Today, Lake Street is the busy northern conclusion of Lake Washington Boulevard Northeast.

Pig Racing

By the end of World War II, Seattle was booming but Kirkland was losing population. It needed to promote itself better. The Kirkland Chamber of Commerce began by advertising the town as a bedroom community convenient to the larger city on the west side of Lake Washington. But city elders also decided that something more fun was in order. Thus was born the Water Carnival of August 1946, the first in a succession of Kirkland summer festivals. Diving and swimming contests were held, along with boat races and a beauty competition. What really drew the crowds, however, including journalists and photographers from around the country, were the Pig Races. With the sanction of the Humane Society (a representative of which pointed out that pigs are surprisingly able swimmers), the race featured 18 porcine paddlers (*above*). They were released from chutes set up in Lake Washington, 75 feet from the shore. Each chute was operated by a bathing-suit-clad lovely, reportedly borrowed from the University of Washington drama department. At the sound of a gun, and with some 6,000 spectators cheering them on, the pigs took to the water. The winner was a hardy hog called the Rose of Normandie (*inset*), who finished the race in 45 seconds.

Index